DUCKS
OF THE WORLD

DUCKS
OF THE WORLD

MODERN PUBLISHING
A DIVISION OF
UNISYSTEMS, INC.

155 EAST 55TH ST. / NEW YORK, N.Y. 10022

Published in the United States of America in 1994 by
MODERN PUBLISHING, a division of Unisystems, Inc.
All rights reserved.

Publishing Manager: Robin Burgess
Project Coordinator: Lynn Bryan
Designer: Kathie Baxter Smith
Map Illustrator: Graham Keene
Editor: Robin Appleton
Photographic researcher: Weldon Young Productions
in conjunction with Terence Lindsey

Typeset in Australia by Accuset Phototypesetting Pty Ltd
Produced in Hong Kong by Mandarin

Book #: 00310
ISBN #: 1-56144-525-8

Front Cover: Carolina or North American Wood Duck.
Tim Fitzharris
Page 1: A Pacific Black Duck.
Graeme Chapman
Page 2: A gathering of Wandering Whistling Ducks.
Tom and Pam Gardner
*Page 3: Social preening plays an important role in the lives of
Lesser Whistling Ducks.*
L.R. Dawson / Bruce Coleman Ltd
*Right: Ducks congregating at the Last Mountain Lake Refuge
in America.*
Stephen Krasemann / NHPA
Page 6: The Mallard shows its glorious wings.
John Shaw / NHPA

CONTENTS

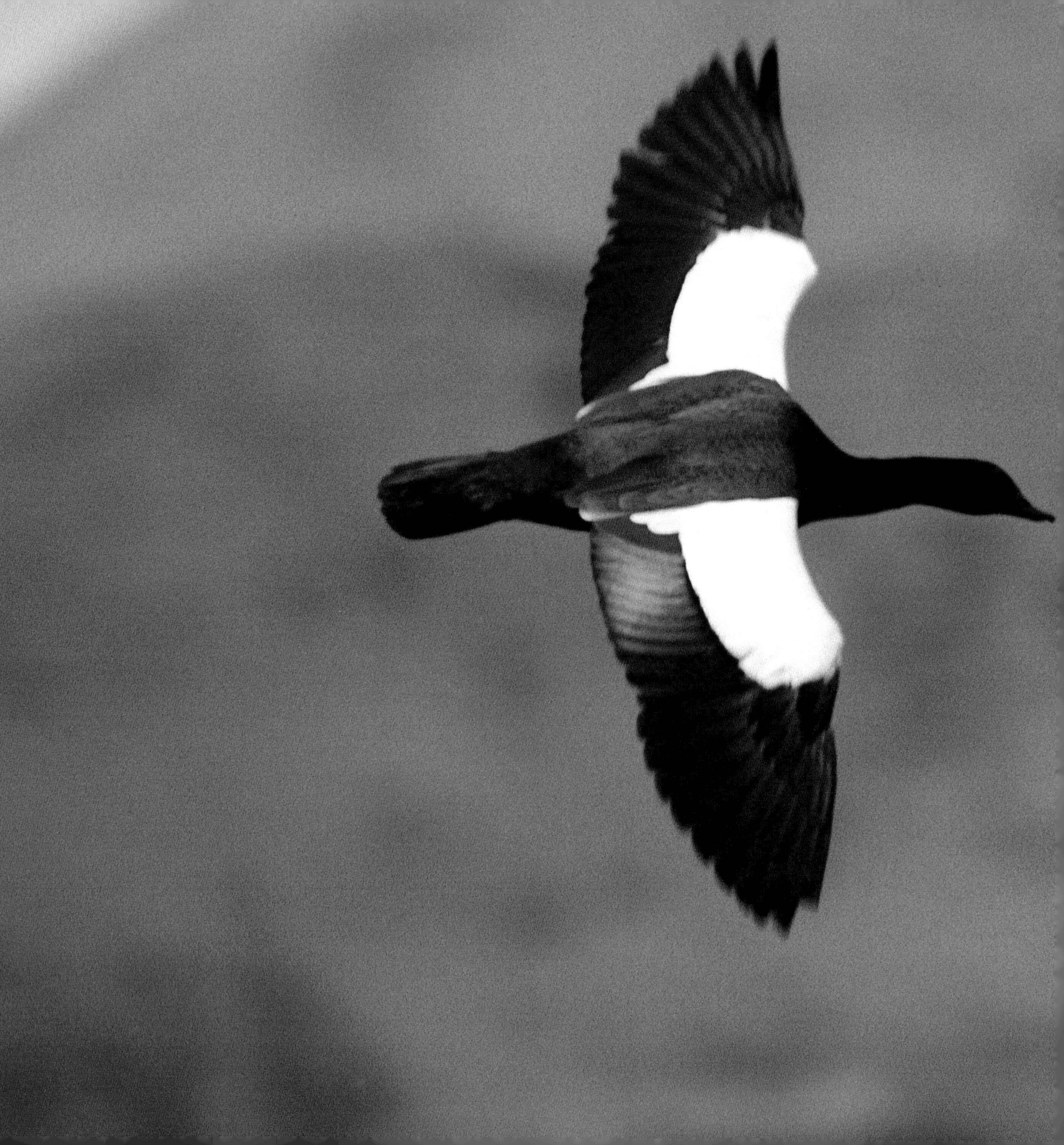
MORTEN STRANGE

Tom and Pam Gardner

INTRODUCTION

The Beauty of Ducks

DUCKS ARE FAMILIAR BIRDS and much-loved by many people, being seen as both charming and useful. Humans are involved with ducks probably to a greater extent than they are with any other group of birds. They were brought into the farm thousands of years ago and, through the Orient and central American regions, became an important part of the rural economy. People have kept wild ducks as pets, or as objects of beauty and interest, exploiting them for sport and food, and conserving them with almost equal enthusiasm.

They belong to the wildfowl family, a group of 145 or so medium- to large-sized birds that also includes the swans and geese. Ducks are found throughout the world in freshwater, coastal and marine habitats, reaching to the high northern latitudes where some, like the Mallard and Pintail, are numerous.

Swans are the largest flying birds and, like their relatives the grazing geese, they have strong pair-bonds and a prolonged family life. They mature slowly and almost always breed territorially, defending their mates, nests, and young ones vigorously. Ducks are smaller than swans and geese, and so they are less successfully aggressive. They are also more variable in appearance and social behaviour. In a few ducks, the male helps to rear the young and has an association with his mate that lasts longer than a few months but, in many more cases, as we shall see, the pair comes together only until the eggs are laid. Parental duties are the task of the female and she is left to guard the ducklings until they are fledged.

Many ducks with helpless young respond to mammalian predators, including humans, not by attacking but by pretending to be flightless, and invite attack upon themselves by giving a 'broken-wing' display. The virtuoso performance of a mother duck, surprised at the pond's edge by the sight of a man, his dog or a fox, suggests that, over thousands of years, birds behaving in this way have left more offspring than those that did not. The mother duck will fly to land and then collapse repeatedly just ahead of any pursuer as if her wings were broken. In a series of apparently narrow escapes, she succeeds in luring the chase away from her precious offspring and finally, the hoodwink complete, will return to her young ones on the water on well-trimmed wings.

Ducklings all hatch with open eyes and with a covering of dense down that protects them from the water. They are able to swim at one-day-old. Ducklings, cygnets and goslings do not hatch with an instinctive recognition of their own kind but, instead, will imprint on and follow the first moving thing that they see. Of course, this is usually the mother, but it can be a member of another family or of another kind entirely, such as a hen or a human. The young find their own food from the start with bills that are broad and somewhat flattened but these differ from tribe to tribe in order to deal, when the bird is adult, with diets as varied as grass, fish and tiny seeds.

Evolution in the wildfowl group has been towards improved adaptation to water-living, so that the birds at the bottom of the family tree are essentially large land birds that can swim, while those at the top are waterbirds that only occasionally come ashore. Ducks are among the more highly evolved of the wildfowl, so their feathers

Page 8/9: The splendid male Paradise Shelduck

Left: A male Rosy-bill with its brilliantly coloured bill.

must provide better waterproofing; unlike swans and geese, ducks renew their body feathers twice a year, and they are able annually to wear two different plumages. In tropical ducks, despite these double moults, the sexes tend to resemble one another but, in almost all high latitude, migratory species, the courting male is brighter than his female who remains as drab as a juvenile for the whole of her life.

The waterproofing and insulating plumage of wildfowl was one reason behind their domestication. The beautiful feathering of adult male ducks meant that in Victorian times, especially, they were favourite subjects for the taxidermist who stuffed their skins, mounted and encased in glass and sold them as decorations for drawing rooms. Duck feathers have also been used on fishing hooks — to catch other animals for humans' food and pleasure. A series of 'wet flies' that to the trout must look like insects at the water surface, have 'wings' constructed of speckled feathers from the shoulder of the Mallard, and the most famous of the series (traditionally the one that catches the most fish) is called 'mallard and claret'.

Almost all waterfowl moult their wing and tail-quills simultaneously once a year and, during the month or so that the next

Above: The Common Shelduck at close quarters is a brilliant **specimen to observe. Left: A pair of Common Shelduck.**

set of feathers is growing, they are flightless, relatively helpless, and more than usually secretive.

The ducks, like other birds, can be divided into taxonomic groupings, or 'tribes', of species that look and behave alike. Some tribes consist of very closely related birds, others of more distantly related cousins. Taxonomy is still not a very exact science and, at times, positions are changed or reshuffled as further research suggests a better arrangement. For this book, I have divided the ducks into 10 tribes.

S. Nielsen / Bruce Coleman Ltd.

Eric and David Hosking

A pair of Pacific Black Ducks at rest.

TRIBE DENDROCYGNINI

Whistling Ducks

THE EIGHT SPECIES OF whistling duck are probably fairly primitive; by that, I do not mean that they are not successful, merely that they show characteristics that are typical of evolutionary stages that came early in the development of the wildfowl from land-based ancestors. Their scientific name of *Dendrocygna* means, literally, 'tree swan' and, despite their small size, they resemble the swans in a number of their behavioural patterns. Confined to the swamps of the tropics and subtropics (to about 35° North and South), a number of species are found over wide ranges.

Whistling ducks have relatively long legs and long necks. Although they are not always associated with trees they spend much of the day perched, in small groups, on the branches of partly submerged trees. They also tend to wade in shallow waters.

Like the swans and geese, but unlike the rest of the ducks, whistling ducks moult their body feathers once a year. The ducks are small. There are seven species ranging on average from 500g to 840g (about 1lb 2oz to 1lb 14oz) in body weight, and the eighth, the Cuban, averages 1 150g (2lb 8½oz).

Male and female are similar in size, with the female being heavier than the male in the breeding season. In this the whistling ducks differ from other waterfowl, except for the stifftails. The size relationship may be to do with both sexes participating in incubation and the frequent choice of small tree holes as nest sites, although the relationship may be the other way around — that they are able to nest in holes only because both sexes are equally small.

The nest site is more varied than that usually chosen by most ducks. The basic condition is probably a bulky, well-hidden nest, built over water with a ramp to it. Nests on the ground, and in tree holes (where they are less substantial because no duck carries nesting material in its bill) are also common, and sometimes structures built in trees by other birds are used. The pair-bond lasts for more than one season, and parents share the tasks of rearing; both build the nest and care for the ducklings — again swan-like characteristics are evident rather than ones associated with most ducks.

Presumably because the eggs are seldom left uncovered, no feather down is necessary to conceal the clutch when the parent is away, and there is no obvious de-feathered area on the breast of the adults, although vasculation of the abdominal skin develops in male and female before incubation. Unlike the young of swans and geese (called cygnets and goslings), the ducklings are conspicuously marked and appear to the human eye to be poorly camouflaged. Their parents seem to help them find food by dabbling beaks-full of seeds in the water, and allowing some of these seeds to leak out to the ducklings which gather around their heads. The ducklings grow slowly on a mainly vegetable diet, and are able to fly between eight and 14 weeks after hatching. Meanwhile many will be lost to predators such as eels and snakes, to accidents, and perhaps to starvation. A dull juvenile plumage is worn for only a few months. They are mature and able to breed by 12 months. Both sexes utter loud whistles which are important in keeping the family and flock together. Apart from the breeding period, the birds are generally gregarious. Mutual preening of the face and neck between mated pairs, and even between flock members, is seen frequently, and it is interesting that a common species of duck head louse is entirely absent from whistling ducks. Food is usually plant material, obtained while diving.

Most whistling ducks inhabit low latitudes where daylight lasts for just over 12 hours, and any seasonal changes in daylength are

Opposite: The Wandering Whistling Duck in flight over North Queensland. Previous page: The Lesser Whistling Duck.

Weldon Trannies

slight. The onset of breeding is determined, therefore, by the arrival of the rains, and regular post-breeding migrations are rare, unless in response to drought. Pair formation occurs after aerial chases, but displays between the male and female (which probably remain together for life) are not conspicuous except after copulation; in those species, like the Fulvous, that mate while swimming, the pair may then engage in a lively step-dance, raising the wing furthest from their partner and treading the surface of the water vigorously. Some birds, such as the Red-bill, copulate while standing at the edge of shallow water after which only an abbreviated step-dance occurs. Threat plays an important part in courtship, and in pair and family maintenance; it involves holding the head down and foward with the bill open and pointing at the opponent, with the feathers of the shoulders lifted away from the body.

Whistling ducks are favourites with aviculturists — the Cuban and Red-billed species were kept in captivity before 1750 — and the Fulvous bred in 1872 at the London Zoo by which date only the Wandering and the Spotted had not been imported. Many of their displays and breeding habits are known through studies of tame birds, and they were described quite early as preferring to keep apart from other ducks. In captivity they will sometimes hybridise with one another but with no other duck species, further confirming their somewhat isolated taxonomic position. In the temperate regions, captive whistlers may lay clutches of eggs at any time from early

Above: Note the plumage of the Plumed (or Eyton's) Duck.
Left: Plumed or Eyton's Whistling Duck

spring until autumn, and presumably only stop then because days become too short to stimulate their sex hormones, or because the temperature becomes too low. In England, they are vulnerable to the cold and easily get frost-bitten toes in winter unless care is taken. They are often the last ducks of the year to hatch their broods; the Fulvous Whistling Duck has laid at Slimbridge as early as 24 February and, as more than one brood may be reared, may lay again in early August and hatch their last clutch in September. In the wild, also, they tend not to have nesting peaks like temperate ducks, unless the onset of the rains is a regular, predictable event; instead, only a small part of the population begins laying at any time.

Surprisingly, perhaps, to those who find them so attractive, large numbers of wild whistlers are shot. In north-eastern Queensland, Australia, for instance, both the Plumed and the Wandering whistling ducks are common game birds, and the Fulvous is hunted in coastal Mexico. They are apparently easy to kill because when one of a pair is shot, the other circles its fallen partner, giving the shooter a second opportunity. In contrast, the range of a few hole-nesting ducks, like the Red-bill, is extended by the provision of boxes placed on trees, and a few species have taken to feeding on agricultural crops or benefit by roosting on permanent water created by dams. So any interaction with humans is not entirely unfortunate.

Roger Wilmshurst/Bruce Coleman Ltd.

SPOTTED WHISTLING DUCK

Little studied in the wild, it is restricted to the East Indies. It is rare and was the last of the eight whistling ducks to be discovered. The naturalist Alfred Russel Wallace collected the first specimen in the Moluccas, in 1852.

In several respects the Spotted Whistling Duck is unlike other members of the group; certainly the feather pattern differs from the outwardly similar markings of the Cuban Whistling Duck from which it can be distinguished, not only by its spotted flanks, but by the flesh-pink spots on its bill. In southeastern lowland New Guinea, birds are seen in pairs and small parties, often spending the day standing on logs half-submerged in the shallow pools in which they feed. At night, larger gatherings fly into the tops of tall dead trees for safety.

Previous page:

PLUMED OR EYTON'S WHISTLING DUCK

The Plumed Whistling Duck bridges the evolutionary gap between the Spotted and the more typical whistling ducks like the Fulvous. Restricted to Australia, it is found along the rivers and among the swamps of the north and north-east. A shy bird, it tends to dabble for seeds and to graze at night. The male and female are the same size and slightly larger than the Spotted variety. Nests are built on the ground in thick grass cover. Because of the beautiful long flank plumes that curve up around the body, it is a popular bird with aviculturists but does not do particularly well in captivity.

Eric & David Hosking

FULVOUS WHISTLING DUCK

*F*ulvous Whistlers occur over a broad range in Central America, Africa, Madagascar, and India without showing any obvious difference except in clutch size, which varies from five to seven eggs in Katanga, for instance, to 10 to 16 in California. The birds are aquatic, and their domed nests are found in clumps of vegetation surrounded by water in swamps and rice fields. They are relatively shy and nocturnal, feeding by diving for grass and rice seeds, and flying mostly at night.

WANDERING WHISTLING DUCK

*I*n size, shape, and its rusty coloured plumage, the Wandering Whistling Duck falls between the Fulvous and the Lesser. It ranges widely over the East Indies and northern Australia. The largest race occurs in Australia, the middle-sized one in the East Indies, and the smallest in New Britain and, originally, in Fiji. It eats seeds and dives more than the Fulvous, giving a little spring upwards before submerging. It feeds at dawn and dusk on waterlily seeds.

Brian Chudleigh

Tom & Pam Gardner

LESSER WHISTLING DUCK

*T*he smallest of the whistling ducks, it occurs abundantly in lowland India and much of southern Asia and the East Indies. The breeding season is long and nests are made in reeds, rushes, and grass on the ground, or in trees and hollow trunks, and even in the abandoned nests of crows and kites. Unlike the rest of the group, they eat snails, insects and frogs.

Dieter & Mary Plage / Bruce Coleman Ltd.

Roger Wilmshurst / Bruce Coleman Ltd.

CUBAN OR BLACK-BILLED WHISTLING DUCK

*T*he largest of the whistling ducks, the Cuban was the first to be described in the scientific literature in 1725, and its name arborea suggests that it was then known to be a duck that associated with trees. It is thought to be an island form derived in evolution from the Red-billed Whistling Duck. It occurs in the Bahamas, Greater Antilles, northern Antilles, and elsewhere throughout the West Indies, but it is rare, having suffered greatly from destruction by the introduced mongoose. In the wild, it nests among reeds or in tree cavities near water.

Tim Fitzharris

WHITE-FACED WHISTLING DUCK

*B*oth males and females of this species have distinctive white face and throat patches, and it is towards these markings that mutual preening is directed. It is isolated from the other species in its evolutionary position. Preening is common and has important social significance in the flock. Highly gregarious and noisy, they live in the wetlands, storage dams, and rice fields of tropical America and Africa. Feeding, mainly on the seeds of knotweeds (wireweed) and waterlilies, is more frequent at night than during the day.

Eric & David Hosking

L.C. Marigo / Bruce Coleman Ltd.

WHITE-BACKED DUCK

Although included until recently with the stiff-tailed ducks, the two races of White-backed Duck (one from East and South Africa and the other, rather smaller and brighter, from Madagascar) are best classified in the same tribe as the whistling ducks. The white back from which they get their name is only visible when the birds take flight, which they seldom do. Pairs and small parties inhabit quiet marshes and backwaters with peripheral vegetation like waterlilies. Male and female are alike; both build the substantial nest in a clump of waterside vegetation, both incubate, and both look after the dumpy little ducklings. The large rich chocolate brown eggs are unique among ducks; perhaps this colour enables the birds to recognise their own clutch and reject any eggs added by other species.

RED-BILLED OR BLACK-BELLIED WHISTLING DUCK

Highly vocal, this duck is found from the southern part of the USA, through most of Central and tropical South America. The southern race is the smaller of the two and has more grey feathers on its breast. Nests are typically in holes in oak and ebony trees, sometimes as high as 10m (33 feet) from the ground. The ducklings have sharp claws and stiffened tails so that they can climb from these cavities soon after hatching, and jump to join their parents on the ground. They are brightly patterned in black and yellow, resembling downy wasps. Their food consists of the seeds of waterside vegetation, including sorghum and millet, but they also graze. The longevity record for whistling ducks is held by the Red-bill — one lived at the London Zoo for over 20 years.

TRIBE STICTONETTINI

Freckled Duck

Graeme Chapman

*T*he Freckled Duck of southern Australia is an oddity with no close relatives. At first sight it looks like a proper duck with rather short legs and large webbed feet that fit it for swimming and wading rather than walking on land. Indeed its nest, which is situated in the hollow of a dense bush, contains large quantities of feather down plucked from the female's breast as incubation begins, just like that of the dabbling ducks. This down enables the bird to cover and insulate the eggs when she leaves to feed and drink, but its presence confirms that the larger male does not help in warming the clutch. However, in some physical features such as the scales on its legs, the bird resembles the whistling ducks and swans, and the downy young is dark grey without any marked pattern — again more like a swan or goose than a duck. The adult plumage, moulted probably only once a year, is oatmealy in pattern, and in both sexes the dark head has a slight crest; the upturned bill of the male duck becomes bright red at its base during the breeding season. So here we have the 'first' duck in which the sexes are dissimilar for that part of the year associated with mating. The parental role also differs as the male does not accompany the brood.

The Freckled Duck is usually found in small flocks on the banks of shallow pools, or in much larger gatherings as the dry season gradually evaporates its wetland habitat. Although its stronghold is the Murray—Darling Basin and the extreme south-west of Australia, it is mobile and turns up in unexpected places if the water environment suits it, and it disappears with the onset of drought. It will perch on fence posts or logs protruding from the water, and has hardly any voice; what sounds it makes have been compared with that of a pig or a toad.

Food is obtained by filtering the surface of the bottom mud, either while swimming or wading, or rarely by up-ending. The diet seems to consist of algae, seeds, and tiny snails. As with so many Australian wildfowl, the breeding season is fixed by the rains. Eggs are found most often between mid-June and mid-September but nesting can occur up to December and

Graeme Chapman

probably at any time. Young birds fly when they are nine weeks old and are in adult plumage at 37 weeks. The species may be declining in numbers; it is threatened by drainage plans and agricultural developments, as well as by wildfowling — a number are shot every season in mistake for legitimate quarry. It would be a tragedy if this peculiar duck were lost through lack of adequate conservation measures.

TRIBE TADORNINI

Shelducks

THE SHELDUCKS ARE GOOSE-LIKE in shape, but generally brightly coloured and unusually (because she does all the incubation), the female is as conspicuous as the male. She nests, under cover in the burrows of mammals, hollow trees, thick bushes, or rock crevices, and the down with which she lines her nest is light grey or white so that it is more easily seen in the dark. Shelducks are social birds but the pairs are highly territorial; they display vigorously and noisily to other pairs before and during the breeding season, and thus they give the impression of being quarrelsome. Indeed, both sexes are aggressive, and the female takes an active part in territorial defence which may be why, unlike most ducks, she is so boldly marked.

Their evolutionary origins are a bit of a puzzle. Except for the Ruddy and the Common, the ranges of wild shelduck do not overlap, and none occur in North or South America. Four of the six species — the Cape, Australian, Paradise, and Ruddy — are clearly closely related and sometimes called the 'Casarca' group. The first three are found in the Southern Hemisphere and seem to have a common ancestor. They possess a temperate-type of breeding pattern in that egg-laying ceases before the long days of midsummer; it seems probable, therefore, that the group evolved in the temperate latitudes, somewhere between 40^0 and 50^0 South. It has been suggested that the Australian shelduck is closest to the ancestral 'Casarca' and that the Ruddy is a recent invader of the north.

The last two shelducks, the Common and the Radjah, are only distantly related and, of the two, the Radjah Shelduck of tropical Australia is the more specialised. Its ducklings are patterned differently and the male's windpipe resembles that of the dabbling ducks. It has a lengthy breeding season, suggesting a long association with the tropics.

Shelducks are not good to eat and, perhaps because of this, they are sometimes protected from being hunted. As they breed at two years of age at the earliest, they are not ideal for 'harvesting'. They can live a long time: one Cape Shelduck lived over 40 years in captivity and, again unusually, females tend to outlive the males. The pair-bond is long-term and both members look after the black-and-white ducklings; nevertheless, females seem to be the dominant partner and, in many winter flocks, outnumber the males. The juveniles in first plumage often resemble their mothers more than their fathers — another feature in which the shelducks differ from their relatives. The two sexes are also unalike in voice, the males whistle and the females utter harsh quacks and growls.

Feeding frequently occurs in sea water at the coast or in saline lagoons, so that the birds take in some salt with their food; they have large nasal glands that extract the excess salt from the bloodstream. Feeding times on the shore are determined by the tides and therefore by the phases of the moon. 'Casarca' birds tend to be grazers and have a more vegetarian diet than Common or Radjah Shelducks which eat molluscs and other invertebrates. Annual moult migrations to places of safety, where wing-quills can be shed and replaced (during which time the ducks are flightless) are common in all species after the young are independent. There are two moults of body feathers a year, so that birds can look different in the breeding and non-breeding seasons.

The name 'shelduck' — which means 'variegated' or 'pied' duck — dates from about 1700. However 'sheldrake' occurs as early as 1325, and it is known even earlier as a personal name (for instance, there was a Roger Scheldrac living in Essex in 1195). In the scientific classification of species by Linnaeus in 1758, the Common Shelduck was pronounced to be *Anas tadorna* — 'tadorne' was apparently an old French Celtic name for a pied waterbird. Myths about the Ruddy Shelduck are common in Indian literature, where the bird's sacred status depends upon the saffron colour of its plumage resembling that of the robes of holy men.

Previous page: Common Shelduck feeding on tiny estuarine snails. Opposite: The beautiful Ruddy Shelduck.

S. Nielsen / Bruce Coleman Ltd.

RUDDY SHELDUCK

The 'rusty' or 'ferrous' shelduck is a beautiful orange and chestnut bird, with a short black bill, pale head, and black legs, wingtips, and tail. In flight, the white patches on the upper and lower sides of the wings are conspicuous. The male and female are similar but they can be distinguished as the female is smaller, lacks the black collar of the breeding drake, and has a white face.

Rare in Europe and Africa but common in Asia, it moves south in winter or to lower altitudes or, occasionally northwards to the coast. It is the only bird in which part of the population nests in north-west Africa yet moves to Europe (Spain) for the winter. Generally, it is an inland, salt lagoon shelduck rather than a marine one. Its diet is omnivorous, including seeds and insects.

Kenneth W. Fink / ARDEA Photographics

CAPE OR AFRICAN SHELDUCK

Named in 1789, when a specimen was shot near the Cape of Good Hope, it is a common bird of Africa south of 19° South. The sexes can be told apart from seven weeks of age because there is more white on the face of the female, and this increases as the bird approaches maturity. When adult, the female Cape shelduck shows considerable variation in head pattern; she can have, at the extreme, an all-white head like the New Zealand species.

The pair-bond is long-term, and territory is staked out on small permanent bodies of water during the dry season.

THE PARADISE OR NEW ZEALAND SHELDUCK

The Paradise Shelduck is the only shelduck that cannot nest in the burrow of a mammal as New Zealand mammals were, until recently, restricted to seals and bats. This duck uses rock crevices on or near the seashore.

The species is unique among ducks as it is the female which assumes a brightly coloured breeding dress — chestnut, while the male is dark grey — although she reverts to grey, in an 'eclipse' plumage, during the non-breeding season. She also has a permanently white head. Female shelducks appear dominant, and the Paradise female appears to be fiercest of all.

Brian Chudleigh

Morten Strange

AUSTRALIAN SHELDUCK OR MOUNTAIN DUCK

Most abundant at sea level, the common name of 'Mountain Duck' is a misnomer. It was first described in 1828 from New South Wales, and this State is still its stronghold. It is widespread in south-east and south-west coastal lakes, estuaries, and offshore islands, where it is shot in some numbers — although its flesh is described as almost inedible.

Graeme Chapman

Drawing by S. Kobayashi

CRESTED OR KOREAN SHELDUCK

(Extinct)

*L*ast recorded near Seoul in 1924, it is now regarded as extinct. This beautiful bird was drawn by Japanese artists 200 years ago and it was apparently kept by aviculturists. When the first dead specimens were obtained, they were presumed to be hybrids. The birds probably nested in Siberia and wintered in Korea, were always rare, with a limited distribution. The Korean was about the size of the Common Shelduck, and the male had a grey body, dark green breast and crown, and a drooping crest. The female, like other shelducks, had white on her head — in this case in the form of pale 'spectacles' around her eyes.

Roger Wilmshurst / Bruce Coleman Ltd.

COMMON OR NORTHERN SHELDUCK

Feeding like a wader and nesting like a rabbit is one description of the Common Shelduck. The introduction of the rabbit to Britain was the greatest boon, and almost 100 per cent of the Scottish Shelduck population, for instance, now nests in rabbit burrows. The main food item, a tiny estuarine snail called Hydrobia ulvae, is small for such a large bird, and it is eaten rapidly by the duck moving its head from side to side while sieving water and mud through the fringes of the bill.

Male and female are alike but the male is larger, taller, and longer legged than the female. They are both white and black, with a chestnut breast-band and reddish feet and bill.

RADJAH SHELDUCK OR BURDEKIN
See following page.

Smallest of the group, this is the only tropical shelduck. Male and female are almost indistinguishable.

It was first described in 1828 when a specimen was obtained in Buru, west of New Guinea. There are two races (that differ in size and the colour of the back plumage) which intergrade in southern New Guinea; the larger of the two is found in tropical Australia, mostly in coastal mangrove swamps and on mudflats. The Radjah feeds by moving its head from side to side with the bill tip just beneath the surface of the mud, taking in tiny organisms. It also up-ends and dabbles, and stamps its feet on wet ground as waders do.

Unlike most shelducks, it perches in trees, and the nest is normally off the ground in a tree hole.

TRIBE TACHYERINI

Steamer Ducks

THE STEAMER DUCKS OF South America are large and heavily built, and three of the four species are almost flightless. Their common name is derived from their habit, when they are pursued, of 'steaming' across the water paddling furiously and churning the surface like a paddle-steamer.

Distantly related to the shelducks, Steamer ducks seem to be the Southern Hemisphere equivalents of the Eiders. They fill a similar coastal niche and, like the latter, they feed on molluscs and other marine invertebrates. Gizzards are large and muscular so that they can deal with mussels, snails, crabs, and clams. As in all other ducks, grit is taken in to grind this food down to a suitable size for digestion. They are good divers, even as ducklings, and adults renew their plumage two or three times a year. Male and female are alike, although the male is larger and often has a whiter head in the breeding season. Sexual maturity is reached after two or three years of age and, once mated, the pair have a long-term bond, so that both look after the young although it is only the female that incubates the clutch. Because of the abbreviated wings, neither sex broods the ducklings, which instead huddle together for warmth.

The four species, one of which was only recently discovered, are comparable in appearance — indeed, they are probably the most difficult of all ducks to tell apart in the field — and they superficially resemble large, grey domestic Mallard. Voices differ between the sexes but not much between the species; all males produce a loud whistle and the females emit a rasping growl. They are aggressive to their own kind, like the shelducks, and highly territorial in defending a length of coastline during most of the year, doing battle with their rivals by hitting out with hard knobs on the 'wrists' of their wings.

The phenomenon of flightnessness is interesting. Why does a bird 'give up' such a valuable asset as its ability to fly away from its enemies and from inclement weather? Presumably there are other compensating advantages that come from retaining the juvenile condition of flightlessness. Nutritionally, the time of fledging is hazardous, since large amounts of protein and energy, and therefore of food, are needed to form the huge flight muscles; these muscles need be developed only if there are plenty of predators to cause a problem, or migration is necessary because the climate varies significantly. Foxes seem to be the only real danger to adult mainland steamers, and they can usually be evaded by the ducks running to the water.

Opposite: The male Falkland Flightless Steamer Duck.

Kenneth W. Fink / ARDEA Photographics

M. P. Kahl / VIREO

FLYING STEAMER DUCK

Darkest, smallest, and most primitive of the steamer ducks, it is also the most widespread. It inhabits southern South America and the Falkland Islands breeding on inland freshwater lakes and wintering on the shore. It is found in pairs and family parties, although larger flocks of non-breeding and moulting birds assemble at times (this species becomes flightless during the wing-moult).

D. & M. Zimmerman / VIREO

MAGELLANIC FLIGHTLESS STEAMER DUCK

Greyest and largest of the steamers, the male is the largest duck of all and he can weigh up to 6 500g (up to 14lb 4oz). Male and female look alike, although the female is smaller. Both have stout orange bills. Confined to the coasts of Chile and Argentina south of 40° South, they rarely form flocks, even while moulting. They feed by diving over kelp beds and, although they have large nasal glands to rid themselves of excess salt, they prefer to drink fresh water from streams running into the sea.

D. & M. Zimmerman / VIREO

WHITE-HEADED FLIGHTLESS STEAMER DUCK

Described as recently as 1981, this steamer is known only from the coast of Chubut in Argentina (about 44° to 45° South) where it had been observed, filmed, and puzzled over for some years. Only the male has the white head from which the species gets its name. An abundant duck, it seems to defend territories smaller than those of other steamers, since pairs are concentrated in certain places. It never strays inland but nests on islands and peninsula shores not far from high-water mark. It consumes more crabs than its relatives.

Roberto Bunge / ARDEA Photographics

FALKLAND FLIGHTLESS STEAMER DUCK

*T*he Falkland Island Steamer is similar to the flying species in appearance but it is larger with a heavier head, and shorter wings. It is well distributed around the islands and abundant on some coasts. Pairs and small parties feed by diving and up-ending as the tide ebbs and flows across kelp beds.

This is the species most frequently kept and bred in zoos, despite the fact that adult steamers are aggressive in captivity. They have been known to catch, shake, and kill other ducks and ducklings.

TRIBE CAIRININI

Perching Ducks

THE PERCHING DUCK GROUP contains a 'ragbag' of 15 species as unalike as the tiny pygmy geese which eat lotus buds, the huge Muscovy Duck that is a familiar inhabitant of the domestic farmyard, and the slender Torrent Ducks that are specialised for life in the white waters of Andean streams. Taxonomists have lumped the group and split it in a variety of ways and, undoubtedly, they are not so closely related as members of the tribes we have considered until now. Primarily tropical and subtropical hole-nesters, in more than half the cases the male is involved in parental care. Sometimes if the pair-bond is a long one, the male and female are alike, and the nesting season lasts beyond springtime and through the summer. All moult their body feathers twice a year so, as in the shelducks, there is an opportunity for the birds to vary their plumage in the breeding and non-breeding seasons, and for the drakes to acquire a dull 'eclipse' plumage while they lose their wing feathers and undergo a flightless period.

The first three species of perching ducks — the Muscovy, the White-winged Wood, and Hartlaub's Duck — are inhabitants of the rainforests of different continents; they tend to be secretive and to be well camouflaged among trees. They can fly through the branches, perch with ease, and nest in holes in the tree trunks. Male and female have similar plumage in all three species.

The next three — the Green Pygmy Goose, Cotton Teal, and African Pygmy Goose — from tropical Asia and Australia are small — indeed, the tiniest of all ducks, weighing only about 300g (about 11ozs) — and have the common name of 'pygmy geese' because of their high, shaply tapering, goose-like bills. These bills are an adaptation for feeding on waterlily or lotus buds and seeds. However the birds are not closely related to the true geese of the Northern Hemisphere. Out of their natural habitat, they seem very brightly coloured, but when they float among dense emergent vegetation, their green, white, and buff-coloured plumage is not particularly conspicuous. None of them is well known in the wild.

The Carolina, and its relative the Asian Mandarin, have particularly handsome males. Both sexes moult twice a year, and the males change into a drab, female-like, well-camouflaged dress during the vulnerable period of the annual wing-moult and flightlessness. Both species are temperate in their ranges, and they are thought to be relics of early radiations into the northern regions by other perching ducks, a radiation that was replaced by the more recent evolution of the highly successful dabbling ducks.

The last three perching ducks (not every authority agrees that they are perching ducks, incidentally) are the Blue or Mountain Duck, Salvadori's Duck, and the Torrent Duck. They are specialised for swimming in white water and exploit an insect food supply that, in calmer waters outside the Southern Hemisphere, is taken by fish. They consume bottom-living caddis and stonefly larvae that also enjoy the richly oxygenated mountains streams. In all three, the female lays a small clutch of large eggs, the male whistles and he has no eclipse plumage. The family is raised by both parents on a river territory which is defended against the neighbours and any intruders. These similarities may result from a common ecology and lifestyle, or they may indicate an evolutionary relationship.

Previous page: Two male Torrent Ducks test the water.
Opposite: The male Australian Wood Duck.

MUSCOVY DUCK

The Muscovy is native to tropical Central and South America. It is large — the male is nearly twice the size of the female — and a uniformly iridescent black, except for white wing patches and pinkish bill and facial caruncles. Apparently imported into England in 1550, the domestic bird spread rapidly in France and it is not certain why it was called the 'muscovy'. Perhaps after the Muscovite Company that traded to South America, or because it was procured from the Mosquito Coast of Nicaragua, where its name was originally the 'Musco Duck'.

The Muscovy was probably domesticated by the South American Indians of Peru as a pet: it had sentimental value but it was also useful for its feathers, and rid houses of ants, crickets, and other insect pests. It was sometimes eaten and so were its eggs. Muscovy drakes will cross with females of other domestic ducks that are descended from the Mallard, producing sterile offspring which mature fast. These 'mules' have been bred commercially in France since the middle of the 19th century, and in Israel, Taiwan, Australia, and South Africa more recently. They are lean-breasted birds, the males of which are force-fed for pâté de foie gras; females are kept and killed for their breast fillets — called magrets.

L.C. Marigo / Bruce Coleman Ltd.

WHITE-WINGED WOOD DUCK

Now one of the rarest birds in the world, the White-wing Wood Duck is suffering the same fate as many rainforest animals. It is confined to South-east Asia and has become a threatened species as great parts of its former range are cleared of their trees. It is similar to the Muscovy in appearance, but the male is not much larger than the female, and both have a black-and-white speckled head or — in specimens from Sumatra — an all-white head. Their voice is penetrating. The ghostly, wailing honk is used mainly at dawn and dusk; from their call comes the Assamese name of 'spirit duck'.

Joe Blossom / NHPA

K. W. Fink / ARDEA Photographics

HARTLAUB'S DUCK

A Central African rain-forest duck with a rich chocolate brown body, blue wing patches, and a blackish head that, in the males, also has a variable amount of white. The male and female have a life-long pair-bond and both care for and defend the ducklings.

They are still common in the Congo and Cameroons, but are vulnerable to the wanton clearing of the forests. They prefer to avoid direct sunlight, and spend the day perched on logs near shaded bodies of water.

G. & G. Attwell / Aquila Photographics

COMB DUCK OR KNOB-BILLED GOOSE

*F*ound in the tropical wetlands of South America,
Africa and southern Asia,
they look a little like White-
winged Wood Ducks with their
speckled heads. However, male
'knobbills' are fairly bizarre in
appearance, having black, fatty
knobs that project upwards
from the basal two-thirds of
their bills. This fleshy 'comb'
enlarges before the breeding
season, and must play some
part in attracting a mate — or
mates, since a harem is the
normal grouping in Central
Africa. Males are larger than
females, but both sexes have
iridescent blue-black plumage
on their wings and back (a
smaller South American race
has black flanks as well).

Belinda Wright

GREEN PYGMY GOOSE

An East Indian and northern Australian duck with, in the male, fine black and white pencil markings on the flanks, white cheeks, and a green neck and back. The female is less green and not so distinctly barred, and immatures at first resemble their mother. They call freely, giving shrill whistles in flight and on the water.

Birds live in deep, freshwater coastal lagoons that do not dry out during the non-rainy season and are full of waterlilies. They are never far from the water, but rarely do dive.

COTTON TEAL OR WHITE PYGMY GOOSE

This pretty little duck is found in north-eastern Australia (where it coexists with the Green Pygmy Goose), and throughout southern Asia as a slightly smaller subspecies. It lacks the dark barring of the previous Pygmy goose and is more sexually dimorphic, as well as having a definite 'eclipse', female-like plumage in the male during the non-breeding part of the year. It calls in flight and on the water in a series of whistling, staccato cackles, so that in India one of its common names is 'quacky duck'. Nests are invariably in tree holes up to 10m (33 feet) from the ground or, just occasionally, under cover in buildings, ruined temples, and chimneys.

Roger Wilmshurst / Bruce Coleman Ltd.

AFRICAN PYGMY GOOSE

Strikingly coloured, it comes from tropical Africa and Madagascar; it has an orange breast and flanks and, in the males, a white and green head, and pale orange bill. There is no male 'eclipse'. The bird occurs in Central and southern Africa in permanent freshwater pools, well-fringed with lily mats. It is usually found in small parties. Nests are made towards the end of the rains in tree holes, cliff cavities, or hamerkop (hammer-head stork) nests. It feeds early and late in the day on ripe lily seeds, and rarely leaves the water.

RINGED TEAL

Circular white patches on the upper wings of both male and female give this duck its name. In other respects the sexes are not alike; the drake does not have a dull eclipse plumage, so that the difference between the sexes is permanent. Despite his rather showy dress, he helps look after the ducklings and he is fierce in their defence. The bird inhabits the forests of central South America, east of the Andes, but it has been little studied in the field, most of our knowledge of its breeding behaviour coming from captive pairs.

Tim Fitzharris

CAROLINA OR NORTH AMERICAN WOOD DUCK

The beautiful Carolina of North America's woodlands has not always been so common as it is today. In 1918, there were probably more in collections than in the wild; so, hunting was forbidden under the Migratory Birds Convention between Canada and the USA, and not allowed again until 1941. Pairs are formed in the winter quarters in the southern States of the USA after an elaborate display by the drakes. Male (left) and female migrate together. The female chooses the nest site in a tree hole — or, increasingly, in a box supplied and made predator-proof. After hatching, the young jump down to join her on the ground and she leads them to the nearest water. Adult Carolinas are fond of acorns and other large tree seeds that they pick up from the water's edge.

Morten Strange

John Cancalosi / AUSCAPE International

MANDARIN DUCK

Although clearly related to the Carolina, this most beautiful of wildfowl has a different chromosome number from other ducks and rarely produces hybrids with them.

The establishment of the Mandarin in the United Kingdom as a wild bird has become an epic. It was imported from China before 1745, bred at the London Zoo in 1834 and, in the 20th century, established feral populations. By far the most important was one centred on a collection at Foxwarren Park in Surrey. In 1929 the French aviculturist Jean Delacour had found a large consignment of Mandarin from China in the Paris market, still in their bamboo crates. He rescued nearly 50 survivors and took them, wing-clipped but not pinioned, to England. Six pairs remained at Foxwarren and bred freely; soon they and their offspring spread into the areas around Virginia Water and Windsor Great Park where, today, there are an estimated 5 000 birds. They nest in tree holes in parkland associated with water meadows.

There is still a reluctance by naturalists and birdwatchers to accept the Mandarin as a British bird. It gained official admission to the British and Irish list in 1971 when it had been breeding in the wild for 40 years.

Brian Chudleigh

AUSTRALIAN WOOD DUCK OR MANED GOOSE

South Australian and Tasmanian Wood Ducks or Maned Geese have a female that looks similar to those of the Carolina and Mandarin ducks. Unlike them, the Maned Goose has a pair-bond that is life-long, although the male's plumage is permanently different from his mate's. He has a mainly grey body, a dark brown head, and a black mane from which the common, and the specific name jubata, are derived. The female's voice reminds one of a cat's 'miaow'.

BRAZILIAN TEAL

This forest-living duck exists in two forms, the southern of which is larger and darker, and migrates northwards after breeding. Neither race is well studied in the wild, but in captivity the pair-bond of the Lesser Brazilian Teal seems long with the male staying with his family. He is permanently somewhat brighter than his female, but there could be a male eclipse. The female is very like a female Ringed Teal, but she quacks. The male has a piercing repeated whistle.

Food is obtained by dabbling in the shallows and probably consists of seeds.

Joseph Van Wormer / Bruce Coleman Ltd.

Geoff Moon

Geoff Moon / AUSCAPE International

BLUE OR MOUNTAIN DUCK

Unique to New Zealand, it has no obvious close relatives. It is territorial and, like many other native birds, relatively tame; the male duck will stand his ground and whistle at a human intruder on his 'patch'. Introductions of mammalian predators to the lowlands, the clearing of the bush cover from many streams, the harnessing of rivers for the generation of electricity, have reduced its range and numbers drastically. The present population, isolated in the highlands, is inbred, and becomes more so all the time.

M. P. Kahl / VIREO

TORRENT DUCK

The specific name of the Torrent Duck, of which there are three races, is armata or 'armed'. This comes from the spurs on the wings of both sexes which they use when fighting for possession of a section of a fast-flowing river. Male and female are sexually dimorphic — in all races the female is chestnut-red and grey while the male is variably white, grey, or black. Both have bright red bills, are slender, and have tail-quills that are elongated for use as underwater rudders and for pivots when climbing rocks. Found along the rivers of the high Andes, up to 3 600m (11 800 feet), from Colombia down to Tierra del Fuego in the south, they sometimes nest on ledges on cliff faces from which the newly hatched ducklings jump straight into the foaming water.

SALVADORI'S DUCK

A near-relationship of this duck to the Torrent Duck is suggested by the striped juvenile plumage of young Torrent Ducks. It is like the black barring of both male and female adult Salvadori's. There is a similar shiny patch or speculum (mirror) on the upper surface of the wings that is obvious when the birds fly.

Discovered in 1894, the duck is found sparsely throughout the mountainous streams and lakes of New Guinea. It is little studied either in the wild or in captivity. The bird has a tiny clutch of three or four large eggs. Another speciality is that the female is said to carry her young on her back, a custom normal in some swans but rare among ducks.

TRIBE ANATINI

Dabbling Ducks

THESE DUCKS ARE CONSIDERED to be the most successful of wildfowl since there are more species and greater numbers of individuals. 'Primitive' dabbling ducks are usually tropical and have long pair-bonds and both sexes share parental care. They look alike but such examples are in the minority. More typical and widespread are the *Anas* ducks of the arctic and temperate regions that are adapted to marshy habitats. They breed at higher latitudes than those to which they migrate to spend the winter. In these dabblers, the male is brightly coloured during the period of courtship, and dull brown during the summer and early autumn when wing-feathers are shed and the birds are flightless for a month or so. Whenever the male has this dull eclipse plumage, with the exception of the New Zealand Brown Teal, he takes no part in family life (the Green Pygmy Goose and the Brazilian Teal may be exceptions to the rule). The male Mallard, for example, is devoted to the same female from October to April, but he leaves her as soon as the clutch is laid, and may woo another mate for the following year. A bright shiny patch or speculum is present on the trailing edge of the upper wing of both male and female.

All dabbling ducks are able to breed at one-year-old, and females lay large clutches so that there can be fairly rapid change to gene frequencies in the population. In the migratory species pair-bonds tend be temporary, so that females are able to select several mates in the course of a lifetime. This inhibits inbreeding but it also places a premium on male appearance and displays. Many males are conspicuously patterned, and they have elaborate courtship rituals that are seen every autumn as pair-bonds are being established for the next breeding season. Nests are made usually on the ground where they are screened by waterside vegetation.

The female alone builds, lining the nest with special dark down (unlike the white down of shelducks and hole-nesting perching ducks). This down grows in just before laying, and she alone warms the eggs against patches of bare skin that develop as a result of her plucking feathers from her breast. Even when the nest is in a tree — in the crown of a pollarded willow, or a hollow branch, for instance — most dabbling ducks do not balance so easily on narrow stems as perching and whistling ducks do. The ducklings are not very different from those of the perching ducks, and they are strongly marked with brown and yellow. Although no adult dabbler is particularly heavy — the 39 species vary in average weight from 245g (8½oz) (Hottentot Teal) to 1 170g (2lb 9oz) (Mallard) — some spend part of the non-breeding season on salt water and therefore need functional salt-excreting glands, a feature that normally goes with large body size. They walk well on land and feed, mainly by dabbling and up-ending, on seeds and invertebrates at or near the surface of the water. They dive only rarely and, when they do, they have to open their wings in order to submerge successfully since they lack the short bodies, broad feet, and short tails that are characteristic of the true diving ducks.

Dabbling ducks are closely related; this is suggested by their ability to mate with one another and produce fertile hybrids. Much of their behaviour is also similar: all females have 'decrescendo' calls — a series of individually distinct quacks used to summon a mate — and inciting postures with which they invite those mates to attack other males. In most winter populations of migratory ducks, there are more males than females; this situation arises partly because females are more susceptible to hunters when they have late broods. So every male will not get a mate. Those that are 'selected' usually follow

Previous page: A male Chestnut Teal. Opposite: A male Mallard in flight.

their female back to the place where she was hatched. All these features have significance in 'speciation', and in the evolution of complex male displays and plumages (female and juvenile dabblers tend to resemble one another). Dabbling ducks are usually classified into seven groups — the wigeon, green-winged teal, austral teal, mallards, pintails, silver teal, and blue-winged teal. One or two do not fit into this scheme, and among these is the African Black Duck.

The first of the dabbling duck groups consists of three wigeon, the Gadwall, and the Falcated Duck. Adult wigeon obtain most of their food by grazing short pasture so that they have small bills and rather rounded, muscular heads. The earliest spelling (1513) was 'wegyons'; it and the alternative 'whewer' refer to the far-reaching whistling voice of the male although, in Cambridgeshire, the males were called 'wigeons' and the females — which actually quack — were known as 'whewers'. They were first priced separately by London poulterers, and therefore recognised as different from the wild Mallard, in 1541.

The Northern Hemisphere wigeon are high latitude in breeding distribution and replace one another geographically on the grasslands of Eurasia and North America.

The green-winged teal group have green specula on the wings of both male and female, and they are all small. Included are the Baikal Teal and Green-winged Teal, both of which are dimorphic and migratory, and the South American and Cape Teal, in which the sexes are similar, there is a long breeding season, no eclipse, and dual parental care. The first record of the name 'Teal' (spelt 'tele') dates from 1274 when carcasses were listed at a price of 1½d for two — half the cost of a Mallard — among poultry sold in London's markets. The bird is not known to have been ever called by any other name in English, and the word is said to derive from the attractive 'tutting' sound made by the males in winter flocks. Today, the designation is used for any small duck species — such as Laysan or Grey Teal.

The 'austral', or 'southern' teal are members of a group that provides an evolutionary link between the green-winged teal and the mallards and pintails. Taxonomists assume that the dimorphic Chestnut Teal is the older form that generally gave rise, on the one hand, to the monomorphic Grey Teal via island forms to the north and, on the other, to the partly dimorphic Brown Teal and Flightless Teals of the south. All have long breeding seasons, long pair-bonds and shared parental care.

Most austral teal are isolated geographically, but the Chestnut Teal and Grey Teal overlap in range in Australia, the first being largely a southern coastal duck, and the second a nomadic bird of the arid, unpredictable interior. The Grey Teal is also self-introduced to New Zealand where it coexists with the Brown Teal, and has spread recently because of the provision of elevated nest-boxes, and protection from hunting. The Maori name of *tete* (pronounced *te-te*) is similar to the Old English 'tele', and presumably also imitates the 'laughing', repeated, call notes of the flock.

The mallards make up a closely linked family with worldwide distribution, and are among the best known of wildfowl. They tend to replace one another geographically; the main ones are the true Mallards of the Northern Hemisphere, the Spot-billed Ducks of Asia, the Black and Grey Ducks of Australasia, and the Yellow-billed Ducks of Africa, while the North American Black Duck, the Philippine Duck and the rare Meller's Duck of Madagascar exist in smaller, more restricted populations. Although the male and female look alike in most cases, the male takes no part in family life. The names 'Black' and 'Grey' are given to a number of them but these labels are a bit misleading as birds are generally brown.

The taxonomy of the Mallard itself is not easy. A large, relatively small-billed, dimorphic race is resident on the southern coasts of Greenland, where it is particularly tolerant of salt water. A small, partially dimorphic subspecies, called by the native name of 'Koloa', is confined to the Hawaiian Islands, and it has become extremely rare because of the introduction of predatory mammals. Two monomorphic races were originally isolated geographically in eastern and southern parts of North America; environment changes and people's relocations of game birds means that they now hybridise with one another, and with the Mallards that are spreading from the north, and they are becoming harder and harder to define and recognise. The Mexican Duck was, at one time, treated as a separate species of Central Mexico; introduced Mallards have crossed with it to such an extent that it is now 'down-graded' to a subspecies and is in danger of becoming a mere hybrid. The Florida or Mottled Duck of Florida, Texas, and Louisiana is perhaps the evolutionary link between the Mallard, and the American Black Duck.

The Mallard has been domesticated for over 2 500 years, the Romans initiated the process in Europe, and the Malays in Asia. Ducks, other than wild ones, were not included in lists of poultry sold in London until 1363 (when they were called 'tame Mallard' — the term 'duck' is not seen until 1528), and duck did not become common in the human diet until the 15th century. The Mallard has produced about 20 farmyard breeds in Europe, but many more in south and east Asia where 75 per cent of all domestic ducks are

Eric Soder / NHPA

A male Mallard.

first two being white, and the Khaki Campbell and fawn Indian Runner are excellent egg-layers.

Features of domestication include large size, a reduced number of tail and wing-feathers, flightlessness, rapid maturation, an increased clutch, long breeding season, loss of 'broodiness' (so that the invention of artificial incubation techniques become necessary at an early stage), loss of aggression, a polygamous mating system, and the laying down of abdominal fat. In all cases the male in 'breeding plumage' has retained the curly tail of his wild ancestor.

The pintail group of dabbling ducks consists of four species that occur in every part of the world except Australia. They all have long necks and thus longer 'reaches' than other dabbling ducks, allowing them to gain food from greater depths. The single dimorphic species, the Common Pintail, comes from the highest latitudes, and has the shortest laying season.

Pintails occur in very large winter aggregations, and are among the world's most numerous wildfowl. In north-west Europe in January, 50 per cent are counted on only 13 sites, each of which holds over 1 000 birds. The Pintail will take waste potatoes from harvested fields, but it mainly eats grain and seed and dabbles in water. The two island forms dive more readily for food.

Two species (according to some experts, three) make up the silver or spotted teal of South America and Africa, and these bridge an evolutionary gap between the pintails and the blue-winged teal.

The blue-winged teal group includes seven dabbling ducks that feed in rather different ways; three of the smaller species eat seeds, the others, the shovelers, are small-headed, large-billed birds that filter the water surface for minute floating organisms, mostly of animal origin. This strategy means that they must feed for much of the day, with little time for loafing, and has an influence on the timing of courtship, pairing, and the moult out of eclipse plumage. The 'blue-wing' of the title refers not to the speculum (which is typically green), but to powder-blue feathers on the shoulders of the upper wing.

The Garganey and Blue-winged Teal are the long-distance travellers of the duck world, the first of the Old World and the second of the New. If a small brown duck turns up on freshwater on some remote oceanic island, then it is normally one of these, and usually a Garganey.

The last two dabbling ducks are perhaps more closely related to other tribes — the Pink-eared Duck of Australia to the shelducks, and the Marbled Teal to the diving ducks. Both are unusual in lacking a metallic-coloured wing-patch or speculum.

kept. Those used for egg-laying are usually brown, while pale-plumaged varieties are farmed for their ability to grow and put on flesh quickly. Only five kinds of domestic Mallard have attained any degree of commercial popularity in the West: the Aylesbury, Pekin, and Rouen have been developed for meat production, the

Anthony Bannister / NHPA

AFRICAN BLACK DUCK

Riverine specialists, they are territorial when breeding and defend lengths of river by threat displays and calls and, in captivity, tend to be quarrelsome. Both sexes have hard knobs on the carpal joints with which they can fight; they use their bills to grasp one another at the back of the neck and strike repeatedly with both wings. The more numerous of the three races is common in South Africa; the Gabon Black Duck is found in French Equatorial **Africa, and the Abyssinian race** in Ethiopia and Sudan. They differ in bill colour and in the beige tinge to the pale spots on the dark back.

Male and female are alike in plumage (he is noticeably larger), and they have a year-round bond. Their food is less insectivorous than that of the other torrent-living ducks. Acorns are a favourite item in the adult's diet.

Bruce Coleman / Bruce Coleman Ltd

CHILOE WIGEON

Chiloe is a large island off the coast of Chile at about 43° South, and here Wigeon are numerous. Male and female are similar in appearance, although she has a soft-hued version of his green and chestnut dress, and there is no eclipse plumage. They have a long-term pair-bond and the male is whole-hearted in his defence of his offspring. Pairs spend much time displaying, calling (the male has an attractive three-syllabled whistle), and challenging one another in showy but harmless fights.

Eric & David Hosking

EUROPEAN OR COMMON WIGEON

*U*ntil the 1930s, when an eelgrass disease affected their favourite food, Wigeon were mostly inter-tidal. Now they graze salt marsh and inland wet pastures as well, and sometimes take waste potatoes left on the fields after harvest. Male and female form a pair on the wintering grounds and stay together until the eggs are laid. The female alone looks after the ducklings until they fledge, while the male goes into an eclipse plumage before becoming flightless.

The north-west European population of this duck consists of approximately 750 000 birds of which 250 000 winter in Britain. Sometimes very large winter feeding and roosting flocks occur — 40 000 is not unusual.

Tim Fitzharris

AMERICAN WIGEON OR BALDPATE

*I*ts common name refers not to a truly bald head, but to pale creamy feathers on the crown of the male in breeding plumage. The bird nests in Alaska and Canada and winters in continental USA and as far south as the West Indies. Individuals occasionally turn up in Britain in flocks of grazing ducks and cause excitement among the bird-watchers. The American Wigeon is not such a coastal bird as its European cousin. It resorts more to inland marshes, and the whistle of the male is briefer. In both species the pair-bond is short-term and there is no dual parental care.

Tim Fitzharris

FALCATED DUCK

The description 'falcated' comes from the special tertial wing-feathers that curve against the tail of the male in breeding plumage. These resemble the hooked bill of a falcon. The duck ranges widely over north-eastern Asia, breeding in the USSR and wintering in China, Korea, and Japan. In its behaviour it is reminiscent of the Gadwall. It does not graze as much as the Wigeon, and is a more typical dabbling duck, feeding at the surface of the water and up-ending for seeds.

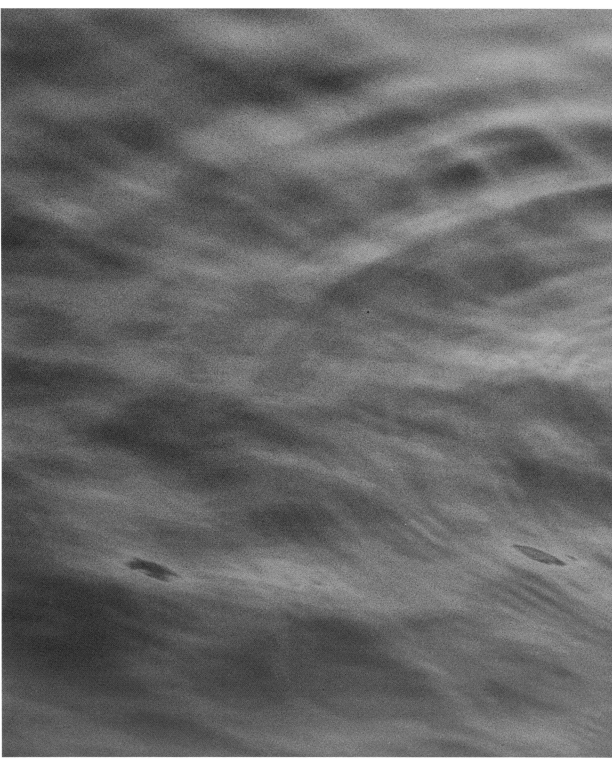

Eric & David Hosking

J.L.G. Grand / Bruce Coleman Ltd.

GADWALL

Gadwall breed over a huge range from Iceland to Kamchatka, across Alaska and Canada, and winter as far south as northern Africa, India, southern China, southern Mexico, and Florida, USA. In Britain, the Gadwall bred first as recently as 1850. It is still rare enough that, although it may be shot, under wildlife protection legislation, dead bodies cannot be sold. A separate, smaller race was at one time endemic on Washington Island in the Fanning Group about 1 600km (990 miles) south of Hawaii, but Coues's Gadwall is now extinct.

Close up, the male is a beautifully patterned grey and cinnamon bird, with white wing-patches and the black under-tail that is common to many Anas drakes.

BAIKAL TEAL

Lake Baikal, the largest lake in the USSR, is not the only or main home of the increasingly rare Baikal Teal. Its scientific name means 'beautiful', and the male in breeding plumage is a handsome creature. There has been a dramatic decline in numbers during recent years, with no large concentrations appearing anywhere in winter except in South Korea. The bird migrates in spring to the far north-east of Siberia, flying through and resting on passage at places such as Baikal. In captivity, it is difficult to breed, requiring the long days that occur only in June in England before being stimulated to mate, nest-build, and lay. The female alone shows parental care, the male moulting into eclipse plumage soon after she has started to incubate.

Erwin & Peggy Bauer / Bruce Coleman Ltd.

Eric & David Hosking

NORTHERN GREEN-WINGED TEAL

The male is a pretty, colourful bird which moults into a female-like plumage soon after eggs are laid; he is not involved in the upbringing of his ducklings.

The range circles the northern pole, one race inhabiting North America and the other Europe and Asia. Teal are among the most widespread and difficult of ducks to count accurately; the population in north-west Europe is an estimated 400 000 and may be in decline because of habitat loss. The European Teal was among the dabbling ducks that could be caught in the 'decoys' used extensively (especially in Holland) to obtain birds for human food from the 17th century, and became the first to have its migration routes investigated by ringing.

S. Nielsen / Bruce Coleman Ltd.

SHARP-WINGED, CHILEAN AND SPECKLED TEAL

Of the four subspecies of the small South American teal, two occur in the northern Andes, one in the Andean region of southern Peru, northern Chile and Argentina, and the fourth is widespread from Tierra del Fuego to 30° South, in the Falkland Islands and in South Georgia. Many members of the southern forms migrate north in winter. The Chilean and Sharp-winged Teal (the two southern races) have bright yellow bills, while the two from the northern Andes, the Merida and Andean Teal, have grey bills. Tame and gregarious, they settle into captivity more easily than their northern relatives, and the male helps to rear the brood. His pleasant trilling voice is heard frequently among the flocks. In the wild, it is a bird of freshwater, taking insects and their larvae, plus seeds, by dabbling, up-ending, and diving.

Roger Wilmshurst / Bruce Coleman Ltd.

CAPE TEAL OR CAPE WIGEON
See following page.

*T*he two sexes of this duck are nearly identical, and the male helps with family duties. They display frequently, and throughout the year. Surprisingly for such an attractive duck, the Cape Teal does not seem to have reached captivity in Europe until 1938.

In the wild, individuals and pairs are scattered, shy and quiet, and they only occur in large flocks when moulting, unlike the Red-billed Pintail which they superficially resemble. Seasonally flooded freshwater and brackish pools are preferred, and Cape Teal typically feed by dabbling with bill and head submerged.

Geoff Moon

GREY TEAL

Four races are (or were) widespread in the Indian Ocean and Australasia where their ecology has been strongly influenced by adaptation to island living. The smallest was restricted to the only large lake on the atoll of Rennell Island, 200km (125 miles) from Guadalcanal. Because of competition with a fish Tilapia, that was introduced into the lake within living memory, this teal is now extinct. It was described as recently as 1942 and was not seen again after 1959.

The Andaman Teal is dark brown with a white eye-ring and, sometimes, a white head. This subspecies occurs only on the Andaman Islands off Burma; it is at home in trees, perching readily and using tree holes as nest sites. A third race, the East Indian Grey Teal, was the first to be described in 1842 and is found in Java and Sulawasi, while the commonest form inhabits New Zealand, Australia, and New Guinea.

The Grey Teal in Australia breeds mainly between 24° and 36° South, and is a mobile, widespread, numerous duck. It is sociable and lively.

C.A. Henley

Drawing by H. Grönvold

MADAGASCAN OR BERNIER'S TEAL

An indigenous duck of Madagascar, it is likely a fifth race of the Grey Teal — it has a similar wing speculum — but is little known, and its nest and eggs are still undescribed. It is another island duck threatened by the introduction of exotic fish into its watery habitat: the plant-eating fish eat out the vegetation, and the fish eat the native insects. The result has been an ecological disaster that is now impossible to ameliorate.

CHESTNUT TEAL

These are sedentary birds of brackish coastal lagoons and the saltwater river deltas of Tasmania and southern Australia. They are not as common inland as the Grey Teal, but they do share with that close relative the qualities of a 'good' quarry duck — that is, they are swift-flying and wary, so that every season, large numbers are shot in southern Victoria and in Tasmania. It is dimorphic — the male in breeding plumage is green-headed and chestnut-sided while the female is brown like a Grey Teal; the females of these two ducks are hard to tell apart.

Graeme Chapman

BROWN TEAL

*F*ound in New Zealand, this duck has an estimated population of about 1 500; it is being bred in captivity and released, largely by aviculturists and wildfowlers working in an organisation known as Ducks Unlimited. It became rare following European settlement. It remained on the shooting list until 1921, despite being tame like many island birds. The first reintroduction of captive-bred birds was to Kapiti Island in June 1968.

The Auckland Islands Teal (right) was the first race of the Brown Teal to be collected and described in 1840. It has much reduced wings and it is essentially flightless, although it uses what wings it has in jumping up coastal rocks. It feeds on invertebrates at night and spends the day among the heaving kelp beds where the sea lions and skuas, which are natural and active predators, are less likely to find it.

A smaller, browner version occurs on Campbell Island where introduced predators have removed it from all but an inaccessible spot called Dent ('tooth') Island. The Campbell Island Flightless Teal is currently the world's most endangered duck, numbering an estimated 30 birds.

Eric & David Hosking

MALLARD

Seen as the typical dabbling duck, Mallard males moult their wing-quills simultaneously and cannot fly for weeks while the next set of flight feathers grows; this process occurs while their conspicuous colours are 'eclipsed'. They spend this time in the company of other males gathered on lakes and ponds for safety from predators such as foxes and humans.

Common throughout subarctic and temperate Europe, Asia, and North America, the female constructs nests in a variety of wetland situations, from the smallest fish pond to lakes and reservoirs.

Tim Fitzharris

M. J. Rauzon / VIREO

LAYSAN TEAL

Laysan is in the north-west of the Hawaiian island chain; it is a narrow islet of raised white coral, only 5km (3 miles) long, with dunes surrounding a central lagoon where the water height varies periodically. Rabbits, put onto this tiny island by fur-traders in the early part of the 20th century, ate down the vegetation on which the moth larvae, flies, **and beetles depend. These** insects are the food of the endemic Laysan Teal. It was reported that by 1930 the duck had declined to the ultimate low of a single female with sufficient semen in her oviduct to replace a destroyed clutch. On several occasions during the early 1900s, less than 10 birds were counted. The last rabbit was removed in the 1930s, since then the population of teal has fluctuated but risen at times as high as 700. The Laysan Teal is presumably very inbred, all individuals being genetically similar if not identical, with no deleterious recessive genes present.

AMERICAN BLACK DUCK

Male and female resemble dark, sooty female Mallards with white underwings and a purple speculum. They feed by up-ending and dabbling but in winter will dive for rooted submerged plants. More territorial than the Mallard, males defend an entire pond while their mates select a nest site, lay, and start to incubate. The Black Duck is confined to well-wooded parts of eastern North America where it was isolated from the Mallard; it has had its range penetrated, and hybrids are now common.

S. Nielsen / Bruce Coleman Ltd.

Eric & David Hosking

MELLER'S DUCK

These resemble russet-coloured female or juvenile Mallards with extra long bills and green instead of blue wing patches. The birds are almost unstudied in the eastern half of Madagascar where they are indigenous and uncommon, although at one time they occurred from sea level to 2 000m (6 565 feet). They are still hunted and may be threatened with extinction. They are named after an English surgeon and naturalist Dr Charles Meller who was Superintendent of the Botanical Gardens in Mauritius in 1865.

YELLOW-BILLED DUCK

One race occurs in Ethiopia, northern Kenya and Uganda, while a paler species extends the range south to the Cape of Good Hope. Both sexes are brown, and have bright yellow bills. They are commonest on freshwater. Their food is about 80 per cent vegetable, and is sieved from shallow water by dabbling and up-ending.

Barrie Wilkins / Bruce Coleman Ltd.

Eric & David Hosking

SPOT-BILLED DUCK

Two of the three races of this duck are sedentary, inhabiting the tropical wetlands of India and Burma, and a third breeds in eastern Siberia, across northern China and Korea to Japan, migrating to winter in southern China and Formosa. Both adult sexes are almost identical. The duck's head has a black crown stripe and another stripe through the eyes. The upper wing surface is brown, with an iridescent green to purple speculum line in front and behind, with black and white bars.

Kenneth W. Fink / ARDEA Photographics

PHILIPPINE DUCK

Derived from a spotbill-like form, it is distinctively coloured. The plumage of both male and female is grey-brown, the cheeks and neck cinnamon, and the head has a dark crown and a dark eye-stripe. Juveniles in first plumage look exactly like small adults. The duck is tropical and non-migratory, endemic to the Philippines and nearby islands, and it lives on inland freshwater pools. Very little is known of its ecology in the wild.

Tom & Pam Gardner

Tom & Pam Gardner

GREY OR PACIFIC BLACK DUCK

An Australasian duck, it is closely related to the Asian spot-bills. Both sexes look like the female Mallard, but have darker plumage and marked black stripes across the sides of the face, one passing through the eye. The female's voice is distinctive; she alone produces the classic 'quack quack' that we tend to associate with every duck, while the male has a softer 'raehb raehb' call that is uttered during courtship. Three races have been distinguished: one is the New Zealand Grey Duck, which is paler in colour than the Australian Black Duck; the smallest is the Pelew Island Grey Duck, which has a wide distribution throughout the islands of the south-western Pacific. All are common creatures of fresh and brackish waters which tend to prefer permanent wetlands to temporary ones. They dabble and up-end for a mainly seed diet but are omnivorous.

Jen & Des Bartlett / Bruce Coleman Ltd

CRESTED DUCK

Long-bodied and long-tailed, this duck has sexes that are similar. Both have a crest of dark feathers at the back of the head, and a bronze-copper speculum on the wing. One race, found at low levels in South America and in the Falkland Islands, (pictured above) has red eyes — the larger one from the high Andes of northern Chile and southern Bolivia has yellow ones. There is also a difference in the down of the ducklings of the two races; the high altitude youngster has long silky plumules. Birds wade, dabble, and up-end in shallow water, in coastal pools, and at the shoreline, taking seeds and invertebrates.

BRONZE-WINGED OR SPECTACLED DUCK

Male and female are alike and the white facial and throat markings and bronze wing-patches are conspicuous. The pair-bond is long-term, and the male stays with and defends his young.

The ducks inhabit streams, rivers and mountain lakes in the wooded parts of temperate Argentina and Chile, from Tierra del Fuego north to about 37°South; a few migrate north in winter but most are resident. The bird has been studied very little in the wild, although it does seem to be tame.

Francisco Erize / Bruce Coleman Ltd.

D. Roby / VIREO

YELLOW-BILLED, BROWN OR CHILEAN PINTAIL

A species which looks like a Speckled Teal, it is larger with a longer tail, and a common duck of Argentina and Chile. There is a second rare subspecies in the Colombian Andes, and a smaller, darker form in South Georgia (from where the species was first described and the original specimens came) at 55° South.

The South Georgia Pintail or Teal (above) is small, lively, walks more easily on land than the Common Pintail, and has a rounded head, a short slightly upturned bill, and a short tail. The wild bird is commonest in the freshwater pools or tussock-fringed tarns near the sea, but it also occurs around the shore. Food consists of fairy shrimps, marine amphipods, and snails.

Roger Wilmshurst / Bruce Coleman Ltd.

NORTHERN PINTAIL

*T*he elegant male wears a
plumage from autumn
until the spring that is
markedly different from that of
the female, while the juveniles
resemble their brown mother.
His two central tail feathers,
from which the whole group
gets its name, are greatly
elongated and pointed, and
lifted over the head in courtship.

Rod Williams / Bruce Coleman Ltd.

BAHAMA (INCLUDING GALAPAGOS) OR WHITE-CHEEKED PINTAIL

This duck is intermediate in form and behaviour between the Yellow-billed and the African Red-billed Pintails. It occurs in the Bahamas and extends in range from the West Indies as far south as Buenos Aires. The smaller of the two 'continental' races is common in brackish water around the Caribbean while the larger subspecies is found in central South America.

The third race of the White-cheeked Pintail is the only duck in great numbers on the Galapagos Islands. The Galapagos Pintail (right) looks like a juvenile of the other subspecies, with less distinctly white cheeks, and a tamer disposition.

P. Evans / Bruce Coleman Ltd.

RED-BILLED PINTAIL

*A*dults and juveniles are alike except that the bill is brownish-pink in the young bird. It is southern Africa's most numerous duck. It is a quiet, undemonstrative and sociable bird of shallow freshwater, dabbling and up-ending, but also feeding on crops, especially at night and after the grain harvest.

SILVER, VERSICOLOR OR PUNA TEAL

There are two major forms of the Silver Teal that are sufficiently unalike to be considered often as separate species. The Versicolor Teal (left) has two lowland races that are brighter in plumage than the less numerous and larger Puna Teal of the high Andean lakes. The northern Versicolor Teal is found from central Chile south to central Argentina, and the darker southern form from the south of Argentina to Tierra del Fuego. Adult males and females are very similar and resemble Bahama and Red-billed Pintails with their pale cheeks and dark crowns. The birds are not well known in their natural freshwater environments, as they are shy, quiet and inconspicuous.

S. Nielsen / Bruce Coleman Ltd.

A.J. Dean / Bruce Coleman Ltd.

HOTTENTOT TEAL

Found in tropical eastern Africa this tiny duck resembles the Silver Teal in its quiet ways, lack of strong voice, and in its blue bill and the dark cap that extends over the eyes. It is easily overlooked in the wild, where it dabbles with bill and head submerged in shallow, well-vegetated swamps and freshwater pools in open country. It never seems to dive for food. The female is slightly less well-marked than the male and has a smaller speculum — often the case in dabbling ducks.

GARGANEY

Known as the only duck that migrates to Britain in the spring to breed, it departs in late summer to spend the winter in Africa. The voice of the male is unmistakeable — a sort of harsh rattle — but evidence of breeding is hard to find, the female is very secretive and she conceals her nest in tall grass within 50m (165 feet) of shallow water. The male leaves his mate during incubation in order to moult his wings, and migrates south in eclipse plumage from late July to September.

John Shaw / Bruce Coleman Ltd.

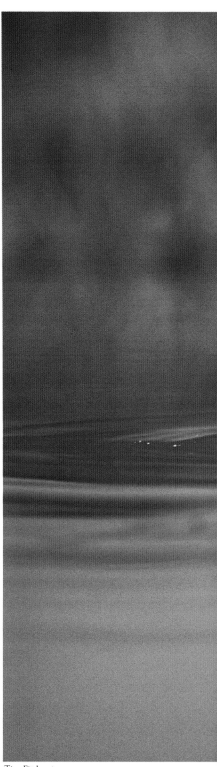

Tim Fitzharris

BLUE-WINGED TEAL

A small duck, it nests up to 60° North in Canada and the USA and then finds a second summer beyond 30° South in South America. It is common in Peru and it occurs as far south as Chile and Argentina. Nests are hidden in clumps of vegetation beside the water and, after an incubation period of 24 days, the mother alone cares for her nine or so young until they can fly at 42 days of age. They eat about 70 per cent grass and sedge seeds, plus small molluscs and water insects.

Bob & Clara Calhoun / Bruce Coleman Ltd.

CINNAMON TEAL

There are five races of the Cinnamon Teal (one in the highlands of western Columbia is rare) that differ in size and the amount of dark spotting on the rusty red plumage of the breeding male. The largest form occurs in the high altitude puna zone, and the smallest form at low altitudes. The race with the darkest spots on its underparts may be found in the wettest part of the range.

ARGENTINE RED SHOVELER

Males have no eclipse plumage (although they moult body feathers twice a year like other ducks) and so they are permanently a much brighter chestnut colour than their brown mate. This duck's bill is wider than that of the Cinnamon Teal and it feeds by filtering the surface of fresh and brackish water for tiny organisms as well as by up-ending for small seeds. It is still unstudied in the wild.

Kenneth W. Fink / ARDEA Photographics

CAPE SHOVELER

The most primitive of the shovelers, this non-migratory duck of southern Africa is also permanently dimorphic, although male and female are neither very colourful nor dissimilar. They are gregarious in small groups on freshwater except when nesting. Feeding may take place by day and by night, and the typical shoveler behaviour of circling together, with necks stretched forwards and bills swivelling from side to side sieving the surface, is frequent. Food may be tiny snails, insects, and crustaceans.

Brian Chudleigh

AUSTRALIAN AND NEW ZEALAND SHOVELER

Of the two races the drakes of the New Zealand form are brighter in breeding plumage than the Australian one, and they breed at a slightly longer daylength. Males of both races have an eclipse plumage that lasts for much of the summer and autumn.

Communal feeding is normal; small groups and pairs circle and sieve the water surface for the small items of food (beetles, snails, and seeds) that they trap with the fine lamellae of their broad bills. The paddling feet of the bird in front will bring up particles that are filtered out by the shoveler following.

Not usually found on salt water, nor in tropical parts; it is one of Australia's rarest southern ducks.

Tim Fitzharris

NORTHERN OR COMMON SHOVELER

This duck breeds as far north as the Arctic Circle and throughout the Northern Hemisphere. It winters to the south, even crossing the Equator on autumn migration. It is the most widely distributed and most colourful of the shoveler group. The English name refers to the broad flattened bill, but the name was originally given to the spoonbill — a relative of the heron. Food is sieved from the water surface and consists of minute water snails and arthropods.

Belinda Wright

Dr Eckart Pott / Bruce Coleman Ltd.

MARBLED TEAL

Currently Europe's rarest duck, it numbers only about 2 000 individuals — all found around the Mediterranean. Male and female are alike — small, mottled, cream-coloured ducks with dusky eye-patches. The nape has long feathers that can be raised into a crest and this is used in display. The bird is not well studied. Its relationship is a puzzle; different authorities have suggested that it is a dabbling duck related to the Cape Teal, the Mallard or the Gadwall, but it has no shiny wing-speculum, and does not hybridise with any dabbling duck.

PINK-EARED DUCK

Pink-eared Ducks look like shovelers. They feed on the surface of both shallow and deep lakes, straining water through the fringing lamellae of their broad, lobed bills. Tiny animal foods make up a large proportion of their diet. They often swim in pairs and small groups, sieving the wake of the bird in front. Male, female and juveniles are alike. The small area of pink feathers behind the eye in adults gives them their name. They are nomadic ducks of shallow waters. Nests are made in tree holes and down is added by the female.

R. Drummond

TRIBE AYTHYINI

Diving Ducks

IN THE 16 SPECIES of diving duck, as in most of the migratory dabbling ducks, the pair-bond between male and female is seasonal, lasting only until incubation starts. Again, there are two annual moults of body feathers and, in general, the sexes look different for part of the year. However, the breeding plumage patterns of the males tend to be less complex than those of the dabblers, and certainly there is no species with a particularly gorgeous male. A shiny speculum is not present on the wing, and iridescent colouring is restricted to the heads of a few species. The divers are a well-defined group of closely related birds — so much so that, like the dabblers, they not infrequently produce hybrids that confuse the birdwatchers. They are better adapted than the dabblers for water-living and, to some extent, occupy the same ecological niche as the swans, but they dive for their plant food (which is their main food) rather than reach for it with a long neck.

A tropical centre of evolution for the whole group is suggested; perhaps the most 'primitive' members are in the genera *Netta* and *Rhodonessa* (the Red-crested Pochard, Southern Pochard, and Rosy-bill, and the Pink-headed Duck) which are not so well suited for diving as the *Aythya* (Canvasbacks, Eurasian Pochard, Redhead, Ring-necked, Australasian White-eye, Siberian White-eye, Ferruginous White-eye, Madagascan White-eye, Tufted, New Zealand Scaup, Greater Scaup, Lesser Scaup) ducks. The former are less specialised in both structure and behaviour, and they inhabit lower latitudes and they feed almost entirely on waterweeds from near the surface of lakes and rivers, although their young require a supplementary diet of water invertebrates, throughout their lives. All are associated with freshwater and they have legs placed far back on the body, large feet, and a lobed hind toe. They have a worldwide distribution. However, nine species have been especially successful in the northern regions where they migrate considerable distances in spring and autumn, and their breeding seasons are concentrated within a short period before mid-summer.

Male courtship display in the divers is less variable than it is in the dabblers. 'Head-throws' in which the male raises his head, sometimes so that his bill points at the sky, are universal. Males of most diving ducks 'preen-behind-the-wing', and rub their quills in order to produce a rattling sound.

Although all diving ducks nest at ground level, they are inclined to build on floating structures, and fashion a base for their nest from emergent vegetation. Egg-laying tends to be later than in dabbling ducks in the same environment, as they need to wait for vegetation to grow, and so they are affected more adversely by drought and drainage. The habit of laying in floating nests prevents predation by mammals such as foxes, mink, weasels, and coyotes. Stranded nests are abandoned frequently by the female. Avian egg thieves, such as crows, are defeated by camouflage and by an overhead screening of reed and grass stems pulled down and arranged carefully by the sitting bird. When compared with the dabbling ducks, diving ducks' eggs are fairly large, and clutches smaller. Like the dabbling ducks, the eggs of the divers hatch after 23-28 days. In all ducks, incubation is shortest in small species that lay at high latitudes, and longest in large species nesting near the tropics. Incubation also lasts longer in hole-nesters than in ground nesters perhaps because the pressure to reduce the period of vulnerability is not so great.

All female ducks will occasionally lay their eggs in the nests of others. In the diving ducks, especially the North American Redhead, this behaviour may be common enough to influence the biology of a local population. At its extreme, the habit is known as 'dump-

Previous page: Red-crested Pochards.

Drawing by Louis Agassiz Fuertes

PINK-HEADED DUCK
(Extinct)

*B*oth sexes had a dark body and lighter coloured wings, but the head and neck of the adult male was an amazingly bright strawberry pink. Described first in 1790, the duck is now extinct. It probably disappeared because of its habitat was reduced as a result of drainage, and it was exploited by sportsmen in India (many of them British) who often failed to observe a closed hunting season. Ironically, the Pink-headed Duck did not even make attractive eating. The year 1936 saw its end, when the last one in captivity in England died, far from its native haunt of Bangladesh.

nesting' and is more likely to occur if there is a shortage of nest sites and an increasing number of birds. A clutch too large to incubate adequately can result.

The phenomenon of an unequal sex ratio is acute in certain diving ducks where females are heavily outnumbered. The imbalance in sexes in the population may be because the female is more vulnerable when she is nesting and rearing young, or more susceptible to wildfowling, or to feeding competition between the sexes.

Many northern diving ducks are favourite quarry for wildfowlers and hunters, especially in North America. The flesh of the Canvasback tastes excellent and over half of their annual deaths is from being shot. Birds come in to roost on a low flight path, and they seem to be peculiarly easy to 'decoy' on to models of their own kind. In general, northern diving ducks have not done so well from humans' agricultural activities as the dabblers have. Because feeding on dry land is not the northern diving ducks' normal regime, they usually ignore harvested grain and potato fields unless these are flooded.

S. Nielsen / Bruce Coleman Ltd.

RED-CRESTED POCHARD

This species has an eclipsed, non-breeding plumage during which the male loses his handsome 'stand-up' crest of orange feathers and, apart from his crimson bill, he looks like a female or juvenile. This and the Canvasback are the largest of the pochards.

SOUTHERN POCHARD ▶

There are two races: one occurs in Africa from Angola to Ethiopa and south as far as Cape Province, while the South American race used to be found from northwestern Venezuela to southern Peru, but the race is becoming rarer.

It is only well studied in Africa where it occurs in small parties. It feeds in the early morning and evening, and loafs on the shoreline for the rest of the day. It walks well on land and, although it does dive for its food, it up-ends more than most diving ducks. The male is permanently darker than his mate, and he has a dark purplish head; the brown juveniles resemble her in having whitish head patches.

ROSY-BILL

An abundant duck, it is found in temperate South America, from central Chile, south to Chiloe Island, and in Argentina, **Paraguay, Uruguay, and northern** Patagonia. The male is unique in having a bright red bill with a bulbous enlargement near its base. The first specimens arrived in captivity at the London Zoo in 1867 and they bred in 1873. Rosy-bills spend much time ashore where they find walking easy. They dive less than other pochards.

Joseph van Wormer / Bruce Coleman Ltd

Peter Steyn

S. Nielsen / Bruce Coleman Ltd.

S. Nielsen / Bruce Coleman Ltd.

CANVASBACK

*I*ts common name derives from the greyish plumage of the male's flanks and back in breeding plumage — it resembles the colour of calico or canvas. The bird's scientific name comes from the waterweed Vallisneria spiralis, on which it feeds. The Canvasback breeds in the western prairie provinces of Canada and in west central USA. It is large, with a relatively long neck, long bill, and sloping forehead. Although it is sexually dimorphic in the winter, the male has a female-like, summer plumage in which he loses his dark reddish-brown head, and is flightless. Drainage schemes on its nesting grounds in recent decades have caused a worrying decline in the numbers of this slow-breeding duck.

Morten Strange

EUROPEAN or COMMON POCHARD

This duck breeds as far east as Lake Baikal, USSR, and winters in the Nile Valley, India, Burma, and southern China. During the last 130 years, it has colonised western Europe, and Britain. It is mobile and moves in relation to food supply and frost. Food is mainly the submerged vegetation of eutrophic waters such as Chara, Nitella, and Potamogeton, but it also takes grain, and introduced invertebrates such as zebra-mussels. The record for longevity among diving ducks is held by the Pochard: one lived in captivity for 20 years.

REDHEAD

The ecological equivalent of the Pochard in western North America, is migratory and takes nearly 80 per cent plant food. It seems also to be closely related to the lighter coloured Canvasback. The Redhead pair needs a 'pothole', often containing alkaline water and 0.5ha (1 acre) in extent, surrounded and invaded by dense vegetation, in order to breed successfully.

Tim Fitzharris

S. Nielsen / Bruce Coleman Ltd.

RING-NECKED DUCK

On the basis of the female's plumage, it has been suggested that this duck should be included in the Netta group of diving ducks; others have regarded it as the New World ecological equivalent of the European Tufted Duck. It is probably more closely related to the Redhead pochards than the courting male's black and white feathers indicate.

The Ringneck breeds in central and north-western North America, where it is especially fond of forest pools, and winters in the southern USA, Central America, and in the West Indies. Its common and scientific names derive from an inconspicuous chestnut collar at the base of the neck of the male in breeding plumage — only visible when he stretches his head.

AUSTRALIAN WHITE-EYE or HARDHEAD

A freshwater duck, it is the only White-eye with no eclipse plumage in the male. One of its two races is found in Australia; the other, the Banks Island White-eye, occurs in Banks and Gaua islands.

The Australian White-eye prefers permanent, deep-water areas with abundant emergent vegetation where its diet is waterlily and grass seeds gained by diving. The species is threatened by swamp and marshland drainage. It is also hunted and numbers in the wild are declining.

Following page: Ducks in Queensland's Daintree Forest, Australia.

C.A. Henley

Weldon Trannies

B. Gadsby / VIREO

E. Duscher / Bruce Coleman Ltd.

BAER'S POCHARD or SIBERIAN WHITE-EYE

The male with his iridescent green head and ferruginous breast, is the white-eye least like the female pictured above. The species is a relic derivative of the white-eye group, perhaps most closely related to the Australian bird, and inhabits the maritime territories of the Ussuri and Khanka plain of USSR and the eastern half of Manchuria. It has been little studied in the wild but it seems to select a more animal diet than the other white-eyes.

COMMON WHITE-EYE or FERRUGINOUS DUCK

It is a temperate, lowland, only partly migratory duck, preferring shallow expanses of freshwater rich in submerged and floating vegetation. It is seldom seen on land, and the female constructs a floating nest which is typical of the group. Only the male in breeding plumage has the ferruginous head, chest and sides to which the common name refers.

NEW ZEALAND SCAUP or BLACK TEAL

These attractive, chubby ducks are sociable birds, flocking in small groups and chirping to one another constantly as they move from one feeding ground to the next. They dive for aquatic plant and insect food for 15 to 25 seconds at a time.

The New Zealand Scaup is a remote island duck that seems to have evolved from a migratory northern form. The male is the darkest of all the diving ducks, with an iridescent purple head, yellow eye, and no eclipse plumage. The female is brown with a dark eye and white band of feathering close to the bill.

Brian Chudleigh

MADAGASCAN WHITE-EYE
(Extinct)

Sadly, this little-studied duck seems to have disappeared very recently owing to the introduction of exotic fish into the large highland lakes, such as Alaotra at 1000m, (3300 feet), that were its only home. The last sighting in the wild was reported in 1970. The male was somewhat between a Baer's Pochard and a Common White-eye in colour, with a dark rufous breast, head, neck, and back; it is likely that it was a race, evolved not long ago, from a Common White-eye stock.

149

Bernd Thies / Bruce Coleman Ltd.

TUFTED DUCK

St James's Park in the heart of London is a haven for two populations of Tufted Duck, resident and migratory, both of which are dependent on food provided by people. The residents were first put there in King Charles II's time, and increased from 12 breeding pairs in the 1950s to just under 70 pairs by 1984, mostly laying in ground-boxes placed for them on the islands.

Two introduced shellfish have been important in helping their spread elsewhere in Britain — the zebra-mussel and Jenkin's spire shell. Mussels up to 25mm (1 inch) long are easily pulled off and swallowed whole by Tufted Ducks.

Eric & David Hosking

S. Nielsen / Bruce Coleman Ltd.

Above: The male Greater Scaup. Below: The female of the species.

GREATER SCAUP

An animal-eater, in North America it is ecologically separated from the smaller Lesser Scaup, and in Europe from the Tufted Duck, by preferring a more marine habitat in winter; it therefore has more active salt-extracting glands. Winter food is the blue mussel which they obtain by diving in shallow, sandy coastal bays.

Dr Eckart Pott / Bruce Coleman Ltd.

Tim Fitzharris

Tim Fitzharris

LESSER SCAUP

The ecological position of the Tufted Duck seems to be taken in North America by the similarly sized Lesser Scaup; it also feeds extensively on freshwater molluscs and the larvae of water insects, and less on plant material than other diving ducks from lower latitudes. A near-relative of the Greater Scaup, which it resembles closely, it is smaller in size and less likely to be found on saline water.

The name scaup first appeared in English print in 1678 as 'Scaup Duck' and derives from skalp, a Scandinavian word meaning 'mussel-bed' — the place where the bird feeds.

TRIBE SOMATERIINI

Eiders

THE EIDERS, BECAUSE OF their habit of diving with half-spread wings, their lobed hind toes, and marine environment, are sometimes classified with the other seaducks, of the tribe Mergini. I feel that they are sufficiently different to be given a tribe of their own. They are unusual in that, when the males lose their beautiful breeding dress after the young have hatched, and before moulting their wings, they adopt a drab colouring that is not particularly female-like; they are black rather than brown, and are still sexed readily even in eclipse. Like most drakes with a non-breeding plumage, however, they take no part in parental care.

There are four species of Eider, one of which has six races, and one extinct near-relative. All are arctic or subarctic in distribution, are marine in winter, and nest on the shoreline. Bulky birds, they take at least two years to reach sexual maturity and resemble the steamers of the Southern Hemisphere. Young females lay later and have smaller clutches and are lighter in weight at the start of incubation than older birds which are, as a consequence, more successful. The ducklings are dark without patterning, and it has been suggested that this is related to the heat-absorbing properties of brown and black — useful for young birds hatching in the chilly arctic regions. They leave their downy nest within a day of hatching and go straight to sea, swimming, diving, and feeding themselves from the start; they seldom go ashore and are almost never brooded, but they can maintain body heat and survive external temperatures of -10ºC for a while. Only in the aberrant Steller's Eider is there an iridescent purple speculum on the wings; the small Steller's Eider is different from the rest of the group in a number of other ways.

The large eiders dive in order to use their strong bills to prise invertebrates, such as molluscs, and plants from the rocks and swallow them whole. Since mussels have been farmed in the coastal waters of Europe and North America, eiders have caused complaints. Unlike oysters and salmon, mussels are not seeded, penned or fed; they are free food for both wildlife and people. The eiders capitalise on an easily obtained food, as the mergansers do at fish farms, and they have become unpopular. In Scotland, licences have been issued to kill eiders.

The displays of male eiders are as elaborate as their plumage, and the cooing sounds that they make are heard throughout the arctic in spring. Most eiders show a tendency to nest colonially and this is obvious on islands or wherever people have provided protection from predators. The ducks, escorted by their drakes, come ashore to prospect for nesting sites in shallow depressions on the ground. The sex ratio is biased in favour of males, so mate-protection is important until it is too late in the season for a female to be fertilised by another drake. The clutch consists of three to five eggs, and the beautifully camouflaged female sits on her nest for 26 or 28 days. In this time she does not eat and she loses one-third of her body weight. Until a predator approaches very closely, she barely moves as movement destroys the effect of the camouflage but, if a potential thief does make her fly, she often defecates over the eggs as she springs away. The gut contents of a starving duck have an appalling odour and, while the droppings are wet, the smell may deter a dog or a fox. After hatching, young eiders tend to creche in large groups in the company of one or two females which give alarm calls if danger threatens; all ducklings respond by remaining perfectly still or diving.

The European and Northern Eider are examples of ducks that have been protected extensively in their wild state, and tamed by humans, for their down. Feather-down, plucked from their breasts by laying females to line their nests, is unique to wildfowl. Its function is to insulate the clutch from the cold and from dehydration, and to camouflage the site while the parent is away. The natural colour of the breast-down is white, but female ducks that lay in the open grow special brownish down at the start of the breeding season so that the nest can be rendered less conspicuous.

Opposite page: The female Common Eider at nest.

The first collection by farmers of quality down is removed soon after incubation has begun; this the duck replaces over the next few days, and the second collection occurs after the eggs have hatched and the ducklings departed with their mother. The down left behind is often soiled and mixed with bits of vegetation, and this requires careful cleaning before it can be sold.

The tradition of collecting down in Iceland has continued for 1000 years. The practice was so important economically that the taking of birds or their clutches for food had to be prohibited.

Eiderdown is unrivalled in lightness, insulating properties, and elasticity. The outer edges of the plumules interlock to provide a dense mass that can be compressed and will spring out again without damage — apparently for as long as 30 years.

Eiders are shot in some places despite appearing to be ill suited for wildfowling since they take two to four years to reach breeding age. They had a special place in the hearts of those who signed the Migratory Birds Convention in 1916 between the USA and Canada; American Eiders were given special protection, as indiscriminate hunting had depleted their numbers greatly and their extinction was feared. The ducks are protected in most of their European range (except in Denmark), and in many parts they are increasing in numbers. In West Greenland, where thousands are killed every year, numbers are declining, and in parts of Canada they are still or again, under severe threat. Eiders are also very vulnerable to oil pollution and thousands have been killed by spills.

Common Eiders have been declining in some other parts of their range, notably Russia, but they have moved southwards and increased in north-west Europe, including the UK.

Jean-Paul Ferrero / AUSCAPE International

COMMON or NORTHERN EIDER

It has six recognised races and is the most numerous of the eiders, ranging widely around arctic and subarctic coasts. The birds differ in size, head and beak colour, the amount of bare skin on the facial shield, and in the presence of short pointed 'sail' feathers on the back.

Stephen Krasemann / NHPA

KING EIDER

The male in breeding plumage has a conspicuous fatty protuberance at the base of his red bill, and a remarkable blue head. Very common around Spitzbergen, Greenland, Canada, Alaska, and off the coast of Siberia, the King Eider probably lives further north than any other duck and is adapted to severe climatic extremes. Breeding success is variable from year to year and adult birds must be long-lived. Only during the breeding season do they come ashore; the remainder of the year is spent at sea and, if they rest, they do so on ice floes. **Adults eat sea-urchins,** sand-dollars and other echinoderms.

D. Langrand / Bruce Coleman Ltd.

Gordon Langsbury / Bruce Coleman Ltd.

SPECTACLED or FISCHER'S EIDER

Rarest of the eiders (with perhaps 200 000 in the world population), it also has the most restricted range. It is still unstudied in the wild, especially in the winter. A striking feather pattern of 'goggles' around the eyes of both sexes is, in the male, white with a surrounding of green; these 'spectacles' are even obvious on the down of the newly hatched duckling.

Drawing by Louis Agassiz Fuertes

LABRADOR DUCK
(Extinct)

*I*ts disappearance may be an example of 'natural' extinction, but surprisingly little is known about it. It was certainly shot and its eggs collected, but probably no more than any other kind of North American wildfowl during the first part of the 19th century. Its curious soft-edged bill suggests that it was a specialised feeder, vulnerable to even the slightest alteration in its habitat. It was said to have been available on the meat markets of New York and Baltimore during the early 1800s but its flesh tasted fishy and it was so unpopular that **carcasses were often left to rot** before they could be sold. The **last specimen was taken in 1875.**

STELLER'S EIDER

*S*mallest (about 860g [1lb 14oz] on average) and 'daintiest' of the eiders, it is the most dabbling-duck-like. Birds rise from the water, producing a loud whistling sound in flight — audible up to half a kilometre (about 550 yards) away when large flocks take off. Otherwise they are comparatively silent; only the females produce a constant low chatter of harsh, guttural sounds. Also unlike the large eiders, the eclipsed male resembles the brown female or juvenile. Feeding dives for molluscs and crustaceans are made simultaneously, with the whole flock vanishing from the surface at the same moment in a cloud of spray.

J. P. Myers / VIREO

TRIBE MERGINI

Seaducks

THESE CONSIST OF THE scoters, goldeneyes, and mergansers. Only the extinct Auckland Islands Merganser, which is thought to have evolved from a northern goosander relatively recently, and the primitive Brazilian Merganser come from the Southern Hemisphere. The seaducks are mostly saltwater divers that are sexually dimorphic in plumage, voice, and display, and they need (unlike most dabbling and diving ducks) two years to reach breeding age. Males, except for those of the Brazilian Merganser, take no part in the rearing of the ducklings. Seaducks are generally silent but, during courtship, males tend to whistle and females to growl. They are fish and shellfish-eaters, which differ from waders in that they do not remove the succulent mollusc or crustacean from its shell before eating, but consume it whole. And they do not cast a pellet of the bones and shells, as some other seabirds do, but pass the lot straight through the gut. They squeeze out and digest the flesh as the meal goes down, and need no extra grit as the muscular gizzard grinds sufficiently powerfully to crush the shells against one another.

Many seaducks are hole nesters, so that they do not breed further north than the tree-line of the steppes. As they cannot fashion the holes themselves, even in the soft wood of a rotten trunk, they must rely on some other agent such as a woodpecker to construct the cavity for them. Other structural and behavioural adaptations are necessary for successful nesting in tree holes. The claws of the female are prominent and sharp for clinging to the bark, and so are those of her ducklings as they will need to climb up inside the nest before launching themselves from the opening towards the ground. Newly hatched young cannot fly, so how do they react when they see the 10m drop? In fact, they leap into the unknown and, being light in weight and covered with down, they tend to bounce and come to no harm.

During research on ducklings within 24 hours of hatching, it was found that their responses depended on where their species normally hatched. Ducklings that first see the light of day on the ground will not jump off an apparently deep 'cliff', while those that hatch in holes in trees, such as day-old Goldeneye and Bufflehead, will select shallow or deep drops at random. However, hole-hatching ducklings do not react as if they could not tell the difference between deep and shallow drops; they run off on the shallow side of the test apparatus and launch themselves with a little jump on the deep one — just as they must when leaving a tree hole.

Seaducks are capable of diving at one-day-old, and young ones of the arctic nesting species are well insulated, with a thick layer of body-fat beneath the skin, a dense downy coat, and a high metabolic rate so that they are thoroughly suited to cold water. The Long-tailed Duck has three annual moults of body feathers, and both sexes have four plumage changes; possibly some other marine divers will be found to replace their feathers more than the twice that is normal for dabbling ducks.

In captivity, seaducks generally live short lives and require special care if they are to survive long enough to reproduce. The Goldeneye has been established as a breeder since 1909, and the Barrow's Goldeneye since 1937, but neither nests particularly freely in waterfowl collections. The Common Scoter nested successfully in captivity in 1971, but the other scoters have never done so. Harlequins bred in 1977, and Longtails in 1971. Of the sawbills, the Red-breasted Merganser and the Goosander have been reared more frequently in captivity than the others. Smew and Bufflehead are extremely difficult to breed and the Hooded Merganser is only a little easier.

Although seaduck are shot for sport, they taste 'fishy' and are

Opposite: Harlequin Ducks.

Charlie Ott / Bruce Coleman Ltd.

relatively worthless on the table. Many are probably killed to protect the sport of fishing and their eggs are still collected for food.

The scoters are dark-coloured ducks that are common around the cold seas of the northern pole. Unlike most other seaducks, the male has no eclipse plumage although the sexes do differ — the male is black and the female dark brown. The name derives from a Yorkshire term for the Common Scoter, and appeared first in an English publication of 1674; the plausible suggestion has been made that 'scoter' was a printer's error for 'sooter', and referred to the sooty feathering of the male.

Charlie Ott / Bruce Coleman Ltd.

HARLEQUIN

This is the only Northern Hemisphere duck found in white water like the torrent ducks of the south. It is a bird of northern North America, eastern USSR, Greenland, and Iceland where, in the breeding season, it takes the larvae and pupae of black fly from fast-flowing inland rivers; in winter the flocks are around rocky shores, feeding on shellfish.

The beautiful blue and chestnut nuptial plumage of the male gives the duck its names: 'harlequin' is a character in Italian comedy who wears parti-coloured tights, thus it has become anything that is parti-coloured and gay, while its scientific name signifies theatrical and dramatic. In winter males, females, and juveniles are dark brown, except for white facial spots. There are two distinct populations of Harlequins, and the Pacific one greatly outnumbers that of the Atlantic.

D. Langrand / Bruce Coleman Ltd.

LONG-TAILED DUCK or OLD SQUAW

*L*ike the Harlequin, this abundant duck is without close relatives among the seaducks. It dives deeper than any others. It regularly goes down 20m (66 feet) and stays beneath the surface for as long as 60 seconds; it is, therefore, caught frequently and drowned in fishing nets — gill-net casualties have been taken as deep as 55m (180 feet). Males dive for longer than females, probably because they are bigger, but females dive more frequently. Winter food is marine crustaceans and molluscs. In the breeding season, it eats freshwater larval insects.

The haunting courtship cry of the male Longtail is a sign of spring in the far north. It sounds rather like 'ow ow owlee', and it is from this that the bird gets its common American name of Old Squaw (although the sex of the performer has been misidentified).

Eric & David Hosking

Tim Fitzharris

COMMON or BLACK SCOTER

One of the two races of Black Scoter breeds in northern Europe and Asia, and the other North American subspecies, which has a much larger patch of yellow on the bill of the male, breeds in north-eastern Asia, the Aleutian Islands, Alaska, and Newfoundland.

It first nested in Scotland in 1855, and in Ireland in 1905. They dive in sandy bays for mussels, other bivalves and sand-eels. The large wintering flocks contain predominantly males, and vigorous displays are apparent as they compete for mates in the spring.

SURF SCOTER

A migratory seaduck of North America, it winters along the Pacific coast from Alaska to California and northern Mexico, on the Great Lakes and also off the eastern seaboard as far south as South Carolina. It is similar in size to the Black Scoter, but has a shorter tail and larger head. Both sexes have massive bills useful for dealing with crabs and clams among the surf, and that of the male is brightly coloured. Like the Common Scoter, the male has a liquid, courtship whistle that is heard in the spring.

Tim Fitzharris

WHITE-WINGED or VELVET SCOTER

Three geographically isolated races have been recognised which differ in the colour and structure of the bill. They are the largest of the scoters, and have white secondary feathers that are obvious on the top and undersides of the wings. The Velvet Scoter is the race that winters around the coasts of western Europe including Britain, the Mediterranean, and the Black and Caspian Seas. It frequently mixes with flocks of the more numerous Black Scoter, but it can be distinguished by the white patches that are conspicuous as individuals rise in the water to flap their wings in display. Wings are kept half-open under the water.

BUFFLEHEAD

*I*ts eggs are laid in nest holes drilled out by a North American woodpecker called the 'Flicker', and so it is confined to the same swampy aspen and lodgepole pine tree communities. It is small in size, a feature that must be determined by the need for the female to enter and incubate a clutch in a relatively constricted space. Outside the breeding season, it favours larger freshwater lakes, rivers, and estuaries, taking shrimps, small snails, and seeds, and does not occur in the massive concentrations of the other seaducks in winter.

In spring it is one of the last ducks to leave for the north. On the breeding ground the male will defend a territory around his mate and sometimes her chosen nest site, and can be quite belligerent to other pairs.

Sam Fried / VIREO

Geoff McCarthy / Bruce Coleman Ltd.

COMMON GOLDENEYE

Females choose a tree hole in which to nest. In Scandinavia, and in belts of coniferous forest across Europe, the Black Woodpecker excavates large cavities but, recently, the extension of the Goldeneye's range has been greatly affected by the provision of nest boxes. Male Goldeneye start courting in September, although pair-bonds are not usually formed until the end of the year. Sessions of display are seen, in particular, when a pair meets a lone male. There are a variety of acrobatic masculine displays; one of the most common is called 'bowsprit-pumping': the neck is extended repeatedly along the water surface, and then withdrawn. The 'head-throw' is also conspicuous and is a rapid performance in which the male's head is tossed back to the rump and held there while a rattling call is given.

BARROW'S GOLDENEYE

The name Barrow's Goldeneye commemorates Sir John Barrow and was first used in 1831 in Fauna Borealis Americana, a book on the animals of North America. They are tree hole nesters in Canada and the USA but in Iceland, where there are no trees, they tend to be low level cavity-nesters. Favourite spring foods are mussels, marine snails, and herring eggs. At Lake Myvatn in Iceland, they do not migrate to the sea in winter but stay in ice-free freshwater within the breeding range.

Following page: A Common Goldeneye hen and her brood.

S. Nielsen / Bruce Coleman Ltd.

S. Nielsen / Bruce Coleman Ltd.

HOODED MERGANSER

When the male is in breeding plumage he is a beauty, with a long, rounded white crest, trimmed at the tips with black, that can be raised in a fan. Courtship display, in which the male leans to his mate with crest erect and utters a rolling trill, is equally showy. His female, also crested, is greyish-brown. It requires the presence of woodpeckers to make its nest holes, and is at home in timberland full of half-sunken stumps and dead trees. It is more of a fish-eater than its relative the Smew, and its bill is finer and longer. The duckling catches fish at one-day old, and instinctively turns them round in its bill to swallow them head-first.

Tim Fitzharris

BRAZILIAN MERGANSER

Among the world's rarest ducks, it was first described in 1817 from specimens taken in Brazil; then for some time after 1922 it was feared to be extinct, but in 1948 it was rediscovered in the north-easternmost part of Argentina. It has never been held in captivity so much of its behaviour is unknown, but recent studies of wild birds suggest that they have the 'primitive' family system of a long-term pair-bond between sexes that look alike and in which both parents tend the young. The male lacks an eclipse plumage. The population is resident and territorial on small fast-flowing rivers that pass through upland tropical forests. The water is clear, well-oxygenated, and full of boulder-strewn rapids. The main food of the adult is a fish *Astyanax* that grows up to 15cm (6 inches) long. Feeding is by diving or by searching with the head submerging up to the eyes.

SMEW

An Old World ecological replacement of the Bufflehead, it needs the large Black Woodpecker to excavate the holes that it uses as nest sites; the duck's range therefore coincides with the same well-grown trees and drowned woodland that the woodpecker prefers in continental Europe and Asia.

Highly migratory, the Smew flies overland to winter on the coasts of eastern Europe, the Black and Caspian Seas, China, Korea, and Japan. The female takes an active part in courtship, and display is lively and noisy. The name 'smew' comes from the whistling sounds made by the male which was earlier known as the 'smee duck'.

Roger Wilmshurst / Bruce Coleman Ltd.

RED – BREASTED MERGANSER

*B*asically fish-eaters, they are slender, long-necked, and expert divers. A few hatching on Windermere in the English Lake District were found to each eat over 20kg (44lbs) of fish in 100 days, so the estimate was that the 131 ducklings reared on average on the lake every year ate 2.6 tonnes (tons) during the summer. The species is commoner on tidal waters, and is more of an estuarine duck than the larger Goosander. It colonised the Lake District only since 1960, and is currently spreading slowly into England and Wales from Scotland.

Roger Wilmshurst / Bruce Coleman Ltd.

Drawing by H. Grönvold

AUCKLAND ISLANDS MERGANSER
(Extinct)

At the time of its discovery by the French Lieutenant Jacquinot, its population was already small. It is clear that the duck occurred in New Zealand since bones have been collected from middens of Polynesian settlers, suggesting that it was hunted out of the mainland by Maoris, and that the Auckland Islands, 500km (310 miles) to the south, were at the edge of its range. Here, many predators — pigs, cats, dogs, and mice — followed the arrival of the explorers. The merganser appears to have taken no evasive action when Europeans 'collected' it. It is a grim fact that, as soon as a bird declined to rarity, the demand by museums for its skins increased. The ultimate reason for this merganser's **extinction may well have been** the relatively large number that was shot by museum collectors during 1901. Today, 26 skins exist in museums. The last pair, killed on 9 January 1902 by a member of staff of the Governor of New Zealand, became skeletons in the Natural Museum at Tring in England.

Norio Yamagata / Nature Production

SCALY-SIDED or CHINESE MERGANSER

A rare duck which Russian ornithologists estimate to number only 1000 pairs, it is, in the breeding season, a territorial bird of forest streams. It is migratory, spending the winter in China and Korea. It is endangered perhaps because of habitat destruction, but the exact reasons are unclear. Possibilities are a shortage of safe nesting sites after the removal of mature trees that contain plenty of holes, and a shortage of food for ducklings and adults because of an altered pH (acidity) of the water. Joint research by Soviet and British scientists is planned to investigate the ecology of the bird in the Russian Far East and to halt, if possible, its population decline.

S. Nielsen / Bruce Coleman Ltd.

GOOSANDER or COMMON MERGANSER

These are large specialist fish-eating ducks whose bills and tongues are adapted for holding slippery prey. The species is divided into three races of which one ranges over the Old World but is replaced in Central Asia by the larger Asian Goosander. In North America, the Common Merganser, as it is called, has a bill that is deeper at the base. At four weeks of age, they can take salmon up to 10cm (4 inches) long. A female Goosander will sometimes take almost the whole of her large family on her back, to remove them rapidly from danger. This happens only during the first few days; later, she may leave her family in the care of another mother.

TRIBE OXYURINI

Stifftails

THE MOST AQUATIC OF all the ducks are the eight stifftails. They are classed in three genera, *Heteronetta*, *Biziura*, and *Oxyura*, although the majority are in *Oxyura*. They are a widely distributed tropical and subtropical group, found on all continents in freshwater and brackish marshes and lakes. They have short, rounded wings, and most have the long stiffened tail that seems crucial to underwater manoeuvring. These tails are often lifted and carried at an angle to the surface, and these are much used in display. Specialised divers, they have legs placed so far back on their bodies that walking is difficult; the three forward toes are large and fully webbed and the hind toe, like that of other diving ducks, is lobed. Their diet contains both seeds and small animals, and these are strained from the bottom ooze of muddy ponds; chironomid larvae are favourites. At about six months of age there is a full post-juvenile body-moult that includes the wings and the tail. The tail feathers, which are used to change direction while swimming beneath the surface, apparently wear out rapidly and need replacing more than once a year. The mechanism whereby tail and wing-quills are shed seems to be physiologically linked — one cannot be moulted without the other. The phenomenon of a double tail-moult could not have evolved if two annual periods of flightlessness had been an enormous disadvantage but, presumably, to these most water-adapted of ducks, any drawback is negligible in comparison with the need for an efficient rudder.

Only male *Oxyura* stifftails have a dull female-like plumage (although the two upland South American races of the Ruddy do not) and they are 'out of colour' for quite a long time. Typically, male *Oxyura* are in non-breeding plumage for much of the year and acquire their ruddy feathers (and a brightness to their blue bills) for only a short period before the nesting season. And there is evidence, especially from captivity, that nuptial dress can be suppressed in subordinate males by dominant, brightly coloured males living in the same pool. Sexual maturity can be reached in one year except in the large Musk Duck which seems to breed only in its second season.

Since stifftails have little need to fly, except during migration, their courtship lacks the aerial displays and pursuit flights that are so common in ducks less specialised as divers. The males frequently produce sounds, not from the windpipe like other ducks, but by using inflatable airsacs under the skin of the throat, or by slapping their feet on the water. They have elaborate displays and, except for the Musk Duck, are sexually dimorphic in plumage. Pair-bonds are short or non-existent, and males take no part in parental duties.

Nests are built over water by the female — often the nest of a coot will be used — and eggs are large, proportionally the largest of all the ducks. From these hatch active, diving, well-insulated young that need relatively little care, even from their mother. For example, the White-headed Duck lays an egg that, at 94g (3½ oz), is between 15 and 20 per cent of her own weight, and she typically produces six in a clutch. The only brood parasite among the ducks is the Black-headed Duck or *Heteronetta* — a member of this group whose offspring receive no attention from any of the adults.

Many stifftails are still not well studied in the wild, and they have been taken into captivity only recently. The Ruddy Duck bred first in a wildfowl collection in the USA in 1935; the White-headed Duck, Maccoa, Argentine Ruddy and Black-headed Duck all hatched for the first time in captivity at Slimbridge in England in the 1970s. In general, the group has the reputation of being difficult for the aviculturist, and the ducklings are particularly hard to hand-rear. Stifftails are summer breeders at Slimbridge, and egg-laying seasons there tend towards the symmetrical pattern seen in the whistling ducks, and in a few other 'primitive', tropical and near-tropical, perching and dabbling ducks: breeding tends to occur before and after mid-summer rather than only in the spring.

A family of Blue-billed ducks.

Graeme Chapman

Eric & David Hosking

BLACK-HEADED DUCK

Found in temperate South America, this seems to be the stifftail most closely related to the other ducks, perhaps to the dabbling ducks, since its hind toe is not lobed, its tail-quills not stiffened, and it feeds frequently by up-ending. It is a true brood parasite, never building a nest of its own but always laying in those of other birds such as Rosy-billed Ducks, ibises, herons, coots, and even hawks. It uses the foster parent only as an incubator and hatcher, as no other care is needed. The duckling leaves the nest as a day-old and, unlike all other duckling leaves the nest at a to attract a parent's attention.

Peter Alden / ARDEA Photographics

MASKED DUCK

*S*mallest of the stifftails,
the male in breeding
plumage it has a black
facial 'mask' on the front half
of its face from which the
species gets its name, and a bill
that is, although slender, the
same vivid blue as in all
Oxyura. The bird is seldom
found in large flocks, but
occurs in pairs and small
parties on freshwater swamps.

RUDDY DUCK ▼▼

O f its three races, the two South American subspecies, the Columbian and the Peruvian, come from high-altitude lakes in the Andes and have lost, or are losing the white 'cheeks' and facial markings of the North American form.

The North American Ruddy has become a most successful Western Palaearctic colonist. The Wildfowl and Wetlands Trust at Slimbridge is responsible for its introduction to Europe. Three captive-reared pairs and one male were imported in 1948 from the USA, and the birds began nesting in the wild in England in 1960.

Francisco Erize / Bruce Coleman Ltd.

David Hosking

WHITE-HEADED DUCK ▶

R educed in numbers possibly because of over-shooting as well as loss of habitat, it is being bred in captivity for re-introduction. Through a scheme organised by The Wildfowl and Wetlands Trust and the Hungarian Ornithological Union, ducks have been raised in captivity in Hungary from eggs laid in Britain, and the first breeding there was recorded in 1986.

The male differs from the brown female in having, in breeding plumage, a bright blue bill (much swollen at the base perhaps because of its large salt-extracting glands); it also has a white head, chestnut breast, and grey and red-brown upper parts.

MACCOA

A resident of eastern and southern Africa, the male in breeding plumage has a back and flanks of bright chestnut, a black head and neck, and a blue bill, while his female is brown throughout the year. Both float low in the water, sometimes with their spiky tails erected at right angles to the body, and they dive to feed. They are usually silent, although the courting male produces a number of frog-like, far-reaching growls and croaks.

Peter Steyn / Ardea London Ltd.

Eric & David Hosking

ARGENTINE RUDDY, BLUE-BILL or LAKE DUCK

A small stifftail that appears to be closely related to the Maccoa of Africa and the Blue-bill of Australia, it is found in South America. The female Argentine stifftail builds a flat, small, grebe-like nest and has a clutch of only three or four eggs.

BLUE-BILL

Found in reedy, permanent wetlands of inland South Australia, the sexes differ in plumage and the male has a long period of eclipse during which he resembles the female and juveniles. They seldom come ashore and feed early and late in the day, spending the rest of their time with bill-tips tucked between the wings on the back. If danger threatens, they dive rather than fly but, if they do take off, they patter clumsily over the surface for some distance before becoming air-borne.

Rob Drummond

F. Kristo

MUSK DUCK

An Australian oddity, it is designed for diving in water up to 6m (20 feet) deep. Its smooth, tight-fitting plumage is shiny like a grebe's, and it has great difficulty in walking on land because its legs are placed far back on its body for use as paddles. Long, stiff tail feathers are used as a rudder when the bird changes direction underwater. The bill is stout, high and rather short and, unlike the other stifftails, the diet consists partly of fish.

The male is huge, weighing about 2400g (over 5lb). He has a grotesque lobe or pouch hanging below his bill which is used in display. The female has similar plumage colour but is only about half his weight. The female feeds her young strenuously for about eight weeks, which is unusual in ducks. Another peculiarity is that the ducklings sometimes ride on the female's back, and even hang on to her feathers with their bills as she dives.

Following page: Pintails in flight.

Paul Daniels

Eric & David Hosking

POSTSCRIPT

IT IS CLEAR THAT ducks are fascinating and beautiful. They are a precious resource, as is their wetland habitat, and both have been wasted during the last century and a half. Wetlands, among other things, filter our water supplies, store excess run-off in times of storm, and act as barriers that prevent damage to our shorelines. They also provide sites for recreation. Yet fens, coastal saltmarshes and lagoons, ponds, lakes, wooded swamps, and bogs have been, and are still being, destroyed through wanton drainage and pollution.

Many birds of remote islands have been threatened during the same 150 years by the introduction of exotic predators that have brought them to the verge of extinction. This has been happening with depressing frequency. Most island ducks are ground-nesters and their eggs make easy meals for introduced animals. In the Caribbean, the mongoose was released in Jamaica in 1872 and has since spread to many other islands; the Cuban Whistler is among the many ground-laying ducks that is as a consequence, listed in the Red Data Book of animals in danger of extinction. The same predator was taken to Hawaii in 1833 to control the introduced rats, but it turned to easy food such as eggs, including those of the native Hawaiian Duck or Koloa. Black rats restrict the Campbell Island Flightless Teal to a tiny inaccessible stack of rock. Cats, dogs, pigs, and armed men pushed its relative, the Auckland Islands Teal, onto the offshore islets of that archipelago and wiped out the unique local merganser.

On the prairies of North America, the numbers of wildfowl, especially the migratory Canvasbacks, have declined along with the potholes or water-filled gouge-marks left by the retreating glaciers of the last ice age. This loss of ducks and their summer breeding grounds had three main causes: the birds were shot by market-hunters and over-enthusiastic sportsmen; millions of hectares of marsh were drained for agriculture and town development, and to those two man-made catastrophes was added climatic disaster — the prolonged drought of the dust-bowl years that withered and dried the potholes. Despite the 1918 Migratory Bird Treaty Act prohibiting sale of shot ducks throughout Canada and the USA, the loss of habitat continued. Then in 1934, Congress enacted a law requiring every wildfowl hunter to purchase annually a 'Duck Stamp', and the proceeds of the sale were directed towards buying and leasing wetlands. At the start of the first season 635,000 stamps were sold at a dollar each; now, over $US350 million has saved nearly 10 million hectares in 440 National Wildlife Refuges. The ducks are not the only beneficiaries — every wetland creature and plant derives protection. Sadly, some American species are still in decline, and the situation can never be restored, since half the wetlands that existed in colonial times have gone forever.

In Britain, a comparable drainage of historic fenland occurred, but no important breeding or wintering duck population is currently decreasing, and this is true of those that are shot in large numbers. Ducks like the Scaup that were affected badly by improvements to coastal sewage works are also returning. Fortunately, many northern wildfowl populations are dynamic; for instance, of British breeding duck species, half arrived and nested for the first time within the last 150 years. Most are self-introduced, but the Mandarin and the Ruddy Duck had assisted passages. The huge increase in new artificial waters — either reservoirs for town water supplies or gravel-extraction pits that are later flooded — has led to an expansion of some types of non-vegetated wetland. The accidental introduction of novel foods, such as freshwater molluscs from other parts of the world, and the large-scale provision of boxes for the cavity-nesters has been beneficial.

In the 1990s, people are more aware of the need to conserve the natural world. An international conference held in Iran in 1971 produced the Ramsar Convention whereby countries 'recognising the interdependence of Man and his environment' undertook to protect their own major wetlands. The results have been encouraging, and

Opposite page: A pair of Shoveler ducks up-ending for food.
Above: African Pygmy Goose in a tree hole.

Peter Johnson / NHPA

reserves have been created and designated (at Bharatpur in India, the Kuskokwim Delta in Alaska and Ouse Washes in England, for example) and protective legislation enacted. On the Farne Islands off Northumberland, the Eiders received a measure of security long ago. Perhaps because their down was useful, St Cuthbert, who died in AD 687, protected them around his hermitage thus creating the first duck sanctuary; locally Eiders are still known as St Cuthbert's Doves or 'Cuddy Ducks'. Other, larger wetland reserves have been appearing in Britain since the 1950s, and a greater proportion of migratory ducks are depending on their safety.

Research ensures that conservationists create reserves in the right places, and helps us understand the consequences of our interference. A series of winter 'Wildfowl Counts', organised by The Wildfowl and Wetlands Trust based at Slimbridge in the UK, and carried out by 1500 volunteers, reports on the numbers of ducks found on about 2000 British waters, and the analysed results are used by conservation organisations to promote refuges or to oppose developments. The information is also used by planners and developers, and by those

John Shaw / NHPA

Above: Male Blue-winged Teal. Left: White-faced Ducks.
Opposite: Gadwall, Shoveler and Pintail in flight.

G Ziesler / Bruce Coleman Ltd.

who need to know the likely effects on duck numbers of recreational activities such as fishing, boating, wildfowling, and windsurfing. Sometimes part of a wild population is trapped and ringed, or banded, so that a long-term study of individual survival becomes possible.

We now realise the dangers of introducing potential predators, such as cats, and food competitors such as trout; hunting is, in more and more countries, controlled within safe limits. The formation of non-government organisations (for instance, Ducks Unlimited in North America and New Zealand, and The Wildfowl and Wetlands Trust in the UK) has helped to focus the public's attention on the needs of wildfowl and their habitats.

So attempts are being made to redress the balance in favour of the birds, and to ensure that human activities are not detrimental to wildlife. I hope that this book, in particular its photographs, will inspire readers to become more involved in caring for their natural heritage, and that future publications will not need to record the extinction of any duck.

Philippa Scott / NHPA

BIBLIOGRAPHY

Anstey, A. 1989. The status and conservation of the White-headed Duck *Oxyura leucocephala*. IWRB special Publication 10.

Barber, J. 1934. Wild Fowl Decoys. Windward House (re-issued in 1954 by Dover: New York).

Bartmann, W. 1988. New observations on the Brazilian Merganser. *Wildfowl* 39:7-14.

Bengston, S-A. 1966. Field studies on the Harlequin Duck in Iceland. *Wildfowl* 17:79-94.

Bolen, E.G. & Rylander, M.K. 1983. Whistling-ducks: zoogeography, ecology, anatomy. Spec. Pub., Texas Tech U. Mus. 20: 3-67.

Brown, L.H., Urban, E.K. & Newman, K. 1982. The Birds of Africa. Vol 1. London: Academic Press.

Buxton, E.J.M. 1962. Courtship feeding in the Red-crested Pochard. *Wildfowl* 13:170.

Campbell, L.H. & Milne, H. 1977. Goldeneye feeding close to sewer outfalls at Leith. *Wildfowl* 28:81-85.

Caspers, H. 1981. On the ecology of hypersaline lagoons on Laysan Atoll and Kauai, Hawaii, with special reference to the Laysan duck, Anas laysanensis Rothschild. *Hydrobiologia* 82:261-270.

Clark, A. 1971. The behavior of the Hottentot teal. *Ostrich* 42:131-136.

Clayton, G.A. 1984. Common duck, and Muscovy duck, in Mason, I.L. (ed). Evolution of Domesticated Animals. London: Longman.

Cramp, S. & Simmons, K.E.L. 1977. The Birds of the Western Palearctic. Vol 1. Oxford University Press.

Darwin, C. 1868. The Variation of Animals and Plants under Domestication. London: John Murray.

Davies, A. 1988. The distribution and status of the Mandarin Duck *Aix galericulata* in Britain. *Bird Study* 35:203-208.

Delacour, J. 1954-64. The Waterfowl of the world. Vols 1-4. London: Country Life.

Dennis, R.H. & Dow, H. 1984. The establishment of a population of goldeneyes *Bucephala clangula* breeding in Scotland. *Bird Study* 31:217-222.

Donkin, R.A. 1989. The Muscovy Duck, *Cairina moschata domestica*. Rotterdam: Balkema.

Doughty, R.W. 1979. Eider husbandry in the North Atlantic: trends and prospects. *Polar Record* 19:447-459.

Dumbell, G. 1986. The New Zealand Brown Teal: 1845-1985. *Wildfowl* 37:71-87.

Earnest, A. 1982. The Art of the Decoy. American Bird Carvings. Pennsylvania: Schiffer.

Einarsson, A. 1988. Distribution and movements of Barrow's Goldeneye *Bucephala islandica* young in relation to food. *Ibis* 130:153-163.

Eldridge, J.L. 1986. Observations on a pair of Torrent Ducks *Wildfowl* 37:113-122.

Erskine, A.J. 1972. Buffleheads. Canadian Wildlife Monograph 4.

Fox, A.D. & Salmon, D.G. 1988. Changes in non-breeding distribution and habitat of Pochard *Aythya ferina* in Britain. *Biol. Conserv.* 46:303-316.

Frith, H.J. 1967. Waterfowl in Australia. Sydney: Angus & Robertson.

Fuller, E. 1987. Extinct Birds. Viking Rainbird.

Gillham, E. 1987. Tufted Duck in a Royal Park. Romney Marsh: E. Gillham.

Grice, D. & Rogers, J.P. 1965. The Wood Duck in Massachusetts. Mass. Div. of Fish & Game.

Hawkes, B. 1970. The Marbled Teal. *Wildfowl* 21:87-88.

Hayes, F.N. & Williams, M. 1982. The status, agriculture and re-establishment of Brown Teal in New Zealand. *Wildfowl* 33:73-80.

Hudson, R. 1976. Ruddy ducks in Britain. *Brit. Birds* 69:132-143.

Humphrey, P.S. & Thompson, M.C. 1981. A new species of steamer-duck (*Tacheres*) from Argentina. U. of Kansas Occasional Pap. 95:1-12.

Johnsgard, P.A. 1961. Evolutionary relationships among the North American mallards. *Auk* 78:1-43.

Johnsgard, P.A. 1961. The systematic position of the marbled teal. *B.O.C. Bull.* 81:37-43.

Johnsgard, P.A. 1965. Handbook of Waterfowl Behavior. Cornell Univerity Press.

Johnsgard, P.A. 1967. Observations on the behavior and relationships of the White-backed Duck and the Stifftailed Ducks. *Wildfowl* 18:98-107.

Johnsgard, P.A. 1978. Ducks, Geese and Swans of the World. Lincoln: University of Nebraska.

Kear, J. 1970. The adaptive radiation of parental care in waterfowl. In, Social Behavior of Birds and Mammals (ed. J.H. Crook). London: Academic Press.

Above: A Red Shoveler among water-lilies.
Opposite page: Low-flying White Pygmy geese, Queensland, Australia.

L. Brown / VIREO

Kear, J. 1972. The Blue Duck of New Zealand. *Living Bird* 11:175-192.

Kear, J. 1975. Salvadori's Duck of New Guinea. *Wildfowl* 26:104-110.

Kear, J. 1977. The problems of breeding endangered species in captivity. *Int. Zoo Yb* 17:5-14.

Kear, J. 1986. Eric Hosking's Wildfowl. London: Croom Helm.

Kear, J. 1990. Man and Wildfowl. London: Poyser.

Kear, J. & Scarlett, R.J. 1970. The Auckland Islands Merganser. *Wildfowl* 21:78-86.

Kear, J. & Williams, G. 1978. Waterfowl at risk. *Wildfowl* 29:5-21.

Kistchinski, A.A. & Flint, V.E. 1974. On the biology of the Spectacled Eider. *Wildfowl* 25:5-15.

Livezey, B.C. 1989. Feeding morphology, foraging behavior, and foods of steamer-ducks (Anatidae: *Tachyeres*). U. of Kansas Occasional Pap. 126:1-41.

Lorenz, K. 1951-3. Comparative studies on the behavior of the Anatidae. *Avic. Mag.* 57:157-182; 58:8-17, 61-72, 86-94, 172-184; 59:24-34, 80-91.

Lowe, V.T. 1966. Notes on the Musk Duck. *Emu* 65:279-290.

Mackenzie, M.J.S. & Kear, J. 1976. The White-winged Wood Duck. *Wildfowl* 27:5-17.

McKinney, F. 1965. The spring behavior of wild Steller Eiders. *Condor* 67:273-290.

McKinney, F., Siegfried, W.R., Ball, I.J. & Frost, P.G.H. 1978. Behavioral specializations for river life in the African Black Duck (*Anas sparsa* Eyton). *Z. Tierpschol.* 48: 349-400.

Madge, S. & Burn, H. 1988. Wildfowl: An Identification Guide to the Ducks, Geese and Swans of the World. Bromely, Kent: Helm.

Matthews, G.V.T. 1974. Anseriformes, article in Encyclopaedia Britannica.

Matthews, G.V.T. & Evans, M.E. 1974. On the behavior of the White-headed Duck with special reference to breeding. *Wildfowl* 25:56-66.

Morten Strange

Above: The Lesser Whistling Duck.
Left: A gathering of Wandering Whistling Ducks.

Meltofte, H. 1978. A breeding association between Eiders and tethered huskies in North-east Greenland. *Wildfowl* 29:45-54.

Mills, D. 1962. The Goosander and Red-breasted Merganser in Scotland. *Wildfowl* 13:79-92.

Mills, J.A. 1976. Status, mortality and movements of grey teal (*Anas gibberifrons*) in New Zealand. *N.Z.J.Zool.* 3:261-267.

Mortensen, H.C.C. 1950. Studies in Bird Migration. D.O.F.: Munksgaard, Copenhagen.

Moulton, D.W. & Weller, M.W. 1984. Biology and conservation of the Laysan Duck. *Condor* 86:105-117.

Murton, R.K. & Kear, J. 1978. Photoperiodism in waterfowl: phasing of breeding cycles and zoogeography. *J. Zool., Lond.* 185:243-283.

Nilson, L. 1974. The behavior of wintering Smew in southern Sweden. *Wildfowl* 25:84-88.

Norman, F.I. & McKinney, F. 1987. Clutches, broods and brood care behavior in Chestnut Teal. *Wildfowl* 38:117-126.

Olney, P.J.S. 1963. The food and feeding habits of the Tufted Duck. *Ibis* 105:55-62.

Ounsted, M.L. 1988. Attempts by The Wildfowl Trust to re-establish the White-winged wood duck and the White-headed duck *Cairina scutulata* and *Oxyura leucocephala*. *Intn. Zoo Yb* 27:216-222.

Owen, M. 1977. Wildfowl of Europe. London: Macmillan.

Owen, M., Atkinson-Willes, G.L. & Salmon, D. 1986. Wildfowl in Great Britain, 2nd ed. Cambridge Univ. Press.

Palmer, R.S. 1976. Handbook of North American Birds. Vols 2 & 3 New Haven: Yale University Press.

Patterson, I.J. 1982. The Shelduck. Cambridge Univ. Press.

Belinda Wright

Payne-Gallwey, R. 1886. The Book of Decoys: Their Construction, Management and History. London: Van Voorst.

Petersen, M.R. 1980. Observations of wing-feather moult and summer feeding ecology of Steller's eider at Nelson Lagoon, Alaska. *Wildfowl* 31:99-106.

Phillips, J.C. 1923. Natural History of the Ducks. Boston: Houghton Mifflin.

Riggert, T.L. 1977. The Biology of the Mountain Duck on Rottnest Island, Western Asutralia. US Int. Dept. Wildl. Mono.

Ripley, S.D. 1973. Saving the Wood Duck *Aix sponsa* through captive breeding. *Int. Zoo Yb* 13:55-58.

Salim, A. 1959. The Pink-headed Duck *Rhodonessa caryophyllacea* (Latham). *Wildfowl* 11:55-60.

Salmon, D.G. 1988. The numbers and distribution of Scaup *Aythya marila* in Britain and Ireland. *Biol. Conserv.* 43:267-278.

Savage, C. 1952. The Mandarin Duck. London: Black.

Sedgewick, H.M. *et al.* 1961. The New Wildfowler. London: Jenkins.

Siegfried, W.R. 1965. The Cape Shoveller *Anas smithii* (Hartert) in Southern Africa. *Ostrich* 36:155-198.

Siegfried, W.R. 1970. Double wing-moult in the Maccoa Duck *Wildfowl* 21:78.

Siegfried, W.R. 1985. Socially induced suppression of breeding plumage in the Maccoa Duck. *Wildfowl* 36:135-137.

Todd, F.S. 1979. Waterfowl: Ducks, Geese and Swans of the World. San Diego: Seaworld.

Vermeer, K. 1981. Food and populations of Surf Scoters in British Columbia. *Wildfowl* 32:107-116.

Weller, M.W. 1968. The breeding biology of the parasitic Black-headed Duck. *Living Bird* 7:169-207.

Weller, M.W. 1975. Ecological studies of the Auckland Islands Flightless

A family of Paradise Shelducks.

Teal. *Auk* 92:280-297.

Weller, M.W. 1975. Ecology and behavior of the South Georgia Pintail *Anas g. georgica. Ibis* 117:217-231.

Weller, M.W. 1976. Ecology and behavior of steamer ducks. *Wildfowl* 27:45-53.

Williams, M. 1979. The Social structure, breeding and population dynamics of Paradise Shelduck in the Gisborne-East Coast district. *Notornis* 26:213-272.

Williams, M. 1986. The numbers of Auckland Island Teal. *Wildfowl* 37:63-70.

Williams, M. & Roderick, C. 1973. The breeding performance of Grey Duck, Mallard and their hybrids in captivity. *Int. Zoo Yb* 13:62-69.

White, H.C. 1957. Food and natural history of Mergansers on Salmon waters in the the maritime provinces of Canada. Fish. Res. Board Canada Bull. 116.

Black-bellied Whistling Ducks.

GLOSSARY

aberrant; abnormal — often a species that is rather unlike the others in the group in which it is classified.

Algae; the family of simple plants that includes the seaweeds.

Anatidae; the family of birds that contains the ducks, geese and swans.

Anseriformes; the order of birds that contains the Anatidae plus the screamers.

arboreal; living in trees.

arthropod; an insect, crustacean or similar invertebrate with jointed legs.

austral; of the southern hemisphere, southerly.

Australasia; Australia, New Zealand and nearby islands.

brood; the young hatched from a single clutch of eggs.

chironomid; an insect that has a aquatic worm-like larval stage.

classification; the ordering of living things into groups that are related.

clutch; the number of eggs laid by a female before incubation begins.

common name; the English or vernacular name given to a species.

copepod; a kind of very small crustacean.

creche; a gathering of young birds from many different families.

crustacean; a group of invertebrates that includes the shrimps, crabs and lobsters.

daylength; the number of hours of daylight in any 24-hour period.

decrescendo call; a call given by many female dabbling ducks consisting of a series of 'quacks' descending in loudness and pitch.

dimorphic; occurring in two forms, often meaning that male and female birds have different plumages.

display; behaviour that has evolved to signal a message to an observer.

distraction display (or broken-wing display); adult behaviour that distracts the attention of a predator from the young by imitating the movements of an injured bird that therefore appears easier to catch.

domestication; the process of taming and maintaining an animal or plant in captivity during which physical and behavioural traits useful to man are selected in the breeding stock, and others are lost.

downy young; a duckling whose feathers have not yet appeared.

duck; a work derived from the Old English 'ducen' which meant to dive, and is related to 'duiken' in Dutch and 'tauchen' in German.

dump-nesting; the laying of eggs by more than one female in a communal nest.

echinoderm; an invertebrate from the group containing the starfish, sea urchins, sand dollars, etc.

eclipse plumage; the dull, female- or juvenile-like plumage aquired by many male ducks after breeding and while they are in wing-moult.

endemic; confined within a defined area.

equatorial; occurring within the tropical regions.

estuarine; occurring in an estuary, where a river meets the sea.

evolution; the process or gradual change, through many generations, by which an organism acquires the characteristics that distinguish it from others.

Family; a taxonomic grouping, such as the Anatidae.

fauna; the animal inhabitants of an area.

feral; a non-native population breeding in the wild but derived from captive stock.

fledging period; the period between hatching and first flight.

flightless period; the period, when adult ducks cannot fly, between the moulting of the wing-quills and their regrowth.

flora; the plants of an area.

form; an imprecise term for a species, indicated by the first part of a scientific name.

gonad; ovary or testes.

Holarctic; the region north of the tropics that includes the Old and New Worlds.

home-range; the area that a breeding pair of ducks will visit while feeding around their chosen nest-site.

hormone; a chemical messenger released into the bloodstream by glands such as the gonads that regulate events such as the moult.

hybrid; an animal or plant whose parents were not of the same species.

immature; non-adult.

incubation; the application by an adult bird of heat to the egg.

instinctive; a behaviour that is not acquired by learning.

invertebrate; a relatively simple animal that lacks a backbone, such as an insect.

iridescent; shiny colour that is produced in the structure of a feather by light refraction.

juvenile; a young bird in the feathers of its first plumage.

larva (plural larvae); the young stage of an invertebrate, such as an insect or snail.

mammal; an animal with fur that feeds its young on milk.

monomorphic; existing in only one form, so that sexes are similar in appearance.

mollusc; an animal from the invertebrate group that includes the snails, mussels and clams.

moult; the shedding of old feathers.

moult migration; a journey undertaken before the wing-moult.

name, see common name, scientific name.

nuptial plumage; the feathering that a bird wears during the courting season — the breeding plumage.

Nearctic; the arctic regions of the New World or North America.

pair-bond; the prolonged association of a male and female.

Palearctic; the arctic regions of the Old World.

plankton; tiny animals and plants that float on the surface of water.

primary feathers or primaries; the outermost, stiffened quills of the 'hand' region of a bird's wing.

primitive; characters that appeared early in the course of animal evolution.

Puna; the dry grasslands of the central Andean plateau.

quarry; birds that may be hunted and legally killed by man.

quill; the stiff feathers of a duck's wing and tail.

race; a population restricted to a geographical area that differs from others of the same species but not to the extent of being classified as a separate species.

raft; a closely-packed group of ducks on the water surface.

relic distribution; a range consisting of isolated populations that may have been joined in earlier times.

ritual display; a display, given to an observer, that is derived in the course of evolution from some non-signalling behaviour such as feeding.

sawbill; a seaduck, such as a merganser or goosander, with a tooth-edged bill adapted for catching fish.

scientific name; an internationally understood name for a plant or animal, always italicised and usually derived from Latin or Greek, that has two parts (for a species, such as *Anas platyrhynchos* which is the Mallard) or three parts (for a race, such as *A.p.wyvilliana* which is the Hawaiian Duck). See also genus.

secondary feathers or secondaries; the inner flight quills of a bird's wing.

Slimbridge; the village in Gloucestershire, England, in which is situated the headquarters of The Wildfowl and Wetlands Trust, and where the widest variety of wild and captive ducks can be seen.

species; a group of potentially interbreeding animals or plants that are geographically isolated from other populations.

speculum; the iridescent coloured patch on the secondary feathers of the wings of (mainly) dabbling ducks and shelducks.

subspecies; see race.

sympatric; where related species inhabit the same range.

taiga; the sub-arctic forest regions south of the tundra.

taxonomy; the study of classification.

temperate regions; those latitudes between the tropic lines and the polar circles.

territory; an area that is defended from intruders.

tropical; occurring within the tropics of Cancer and Capricorn.

Tribe; the subdivision of a family of birds that includes one or more related genera.

tundra; arctic lands between the taiga tree-line and the northern permafrost.

vasculation; the supply of blood vessels to an area, often the skin.

wildfowl; in Britain, a term used for ducks, geese and swans.

Wildfowl and Wetlands Trust; the organisation founded in 1946 at Slimbridge in the UK by Sir Peter Scott to study and conserve ducks, geese and swans, which publishes the scientific journal, *Wildfowl*.

wing-moult; the period during which the wing-quills (and tail-quills) are lost simultaneously and a duck is flightless.

COMMON NAME (Scientific)	HABITAT	BREEDING & WEIGHT
WHISTLING DUCKS (Tribe Dendrocygnini)		
Spotted Whistling (Dendrocygna guttata)		A long season with cavity nests between April — September. Both sexes of all whistling ducks incubate, and all breed at one year old. Av. about 800g (1lb 12oz)
Plumed or Eyton's Whistling (D. eytoni)		September — October in South Australia. February — April in North. Clutch size: 8-14 eggs. Males: 600-930g (av. 789g) (1lb 11oz). Females: 580-1400g (av. 792g) (1lb 12oz)
Fulvous Whistling (D. bicolor)		Lays any time of the year depending on location and rainy season. Multiple clutches, dump-nesting common. Clutch size: 8-16 eggs, usually 10. Males: 621-755g (av. 675g) (1lb 8oz). Females: 631-739g (av. 690g) (1lb 8½oz)
Wandering Whistling (D. arcuata)		May lay year-round, or upon arrival of rains. Clutch size: 6-15 eggs. Males: 866-948g (av. 741g) (1lb 10oz). Females: 453-486g (av. 732g) (1lb 9oz)
Lesser Whistling (D. javanica)		Long season. Breeds in wet season in most of its range. Clutch size: 7-12 eggs. About 450-600g (1lb-1lb 15oz)
White-faced Whistling (D. viduata)		Depends on locality and rainfall. In Zambia: February & March. In Zimbabwe: October & November. Clutch size: 6-12 eggs, usually 7 or 8. Males: 637-735g (1lb 6oz — 1lb 10oz). Females: 500-820g (av. 662g) (1lb 7oz)
Cuban or Black-faced Whistling (D. arborea)		Not well studied. Known to lay from June—October. Clutch size: 11 eggs. Females: av. 1150g (2lb 8oz)
Red-billed or Black-bellied Whistling (D. autumnalis)		Nests from early May—mid October in tree cavities. Clutch size: 12-16 eggs. Males: 680-907g (av. 816g) (1lb 13oz). Females: 650-1020g (av. 859g) (1lb 13½oz)
White-backed Duck (Thalassornis leuconotis)		Nests between November & May. Clutch size: 6 or 7 eggs. Both sexes incubate. Males: 650-790g (1lb 7oz — 1lb 12oz). Females: 635-765g (1lb 6oz — 1lb 11oz)
FRECKLED DUCK (Tribe Stictonetti)		
Freckled Duck (Stictonetta naevosa)		Breeding season is fixed by the rains. Most often June—September but can occur up to December. Clutch size: 5-10 eggs, only female incubates. Males: 747-1130g (av. 969g) (2lb 2oz). Females: 691-985g (av. 242g) (1lb 13oz)
SHELDUCKS (Tribe Tadornini) All shelduck breed at two years old		
Ruddy Shelduck (Tadorna ferruginea)		Will nest mid-March—mid-April in holes in banks. Clutch size: 8-9 eggs. Males: 1200-1640g (2lb 6oz — 3lb 6oz). Females: 925-1500g (2lb ½oz — 3lb 5oz)
Cape or African Shelduck (T. cana)		Egg-laying starts in mid-May and ends late September. Nest often made in mammal burrow. Clutch size: 6-13 eggs, usually 10. Males: av. 1758g (3lb 14oz). Females: 1417g (3lb 2oz)

COMMON NAME (Scientific)	HABITAT	BREEDING & WEIGHT
Paradise or New Zealand Shelduck (T. variegata)		Prolonged — lasting from August to January Clutch size: 5-11 eggs Females: 1260-1340g (2lb 12oz — 2lb 15oz)
Australian or Mountain Shelduck (T. tadornoides)		Takes up breeding territories in March & April; lays from mid-June onwards Clutch size: 10-14 eggs Males: 990-1980g (av. 1559g) (3lb 7oz) Females: 878-1850g (av. 1291g) (2lb 13 oz)
Crested or Korean Shelduck (T. cristata)		Now regarded as extinct
Common Shelduck (T. tadorna)		Lays from early May—June in burrows Normal clutch size: 8-9 eggs Multiple clutches: 14-30 eggs Males: 980-1450g (2lb 2½oz — 3lb 3oz) Females: 801-1250g (1lb 12oz — 2lb 12oz)
Radjah Shelduck or Burdekin (T. radjah)		Lays January — June Nests in tree holes Clutch size: 6-12 eggs Males: 750-1101g (av. 750g) (1lb 10½oz) Females: 600-1130g (av. 889g) (1lb 13½ oz)

STEAMER DUCKS
(Tribe Tachyerini)

COMMON NAME (Scientific)	HABITAT	BREEDING & WEIGHT
Flying Steamer (Tachyeres patachonicus)		In Falklands, breeding season starts in October In Chile, lasts from November—January Clutch size: 5-9 eggs Males: 2892-3175g (av. 3073g) (6lb 12oz) Females: 2438-2835g (av. 2616g) (5lb 12oz)

COMMON NAME (Scientific)	HABITAT	BREEDING & WEIGHT
Magellanic Flightless Steamer (T. pteneres)		Nests September — December Clutch size: 5-8 eggs Males: 5897-6180g (av. 6039g) (13lb 3oz) Females: 3629-4163g (av. 4111g) (9lb)
White-headed Flightless Steamer (T. leucocephalus)		Nests October — February Males: av. 3790g (8lb 3oz) Females: av. 2950g (6lb 7oz)
Falkland Flightless Steamer (T. brachypterus)		Laying from mid-September — late December Clutch size: 5-8 eggs Males: 4303-4420g (9½lb-9lb 6oz) Females: av. 3400g (7lb 5oz)

PERCHING DUCKS
(Tribe Cairinini)

COMMON NAME (Scientific)	HABITAT	BREEDING & WEIGHT
Muscovy (Cairina moschata)		In the wild, lays at anytime; in captivity in UK, early spring, through mid-summer to autumn Hole-nester Clutch size: 8-15 eggs Males: 2-4kg (4lb 6oz-8lb 12oz) Females: 1.1-1.5kg (2lb 6½oz-3lb 5oz)
White-winged Wood Duck (C. scutulata)		Rare. Breeding programmes are underway in many zoos. Springtime breeders. Cavity-nesters Clutch size: 6-13 eggs in captivity Males: 2945-3855g (6lb 7½oz — 8lb 3oz) Females: 1925-3050g (4lb 4oz — 6lb 14oz)
Hartlaub's Duck (C. [Pteronetta] hartlaubi)		A nest in the wild has never been studied. Cavity-nester in captivity Clutch size: 7-11 eggs in captivity Both sexes: 800-940g (1lb 12oz — 2lb 1oz)

COMMON NAME (Scientific)	HABITAT	BREEDING & WEIGHT
Comb Duck or Knob-billed Goose (Sarkidiornis melanotos)		Nests in wet season Clutch size: 8-12 eggs Males: 1300-2610g (2lb 13½oz — 5lb 8½oz) Females: 1230-2325g (2lb 11oz — 5lb 1½oz)
Green Pygmy Goose (Nettapus pulchellus)		Nests in wet season in cavities Clutch size: 8-12 eggs Males: 300-430g (av. 310g) (11oz) Females: 245-340g (av. 304g) (11oz)
Cotton Teal or White Pygmy Goose (N. coromandelianus)		Nests in wet season in cavities Concentrated between July—August Clutch size: 6-15 eggs Males: 311-430g (av. 403g) (14.2oz) Females: 255-439g (av. 380g) (13½oz)
African Pygmy Goose (N. auritus)		Nests constructed towards the end of the rains, in tree hollows off the ground Clutch size: 6-12 eggs Males: 285g (10oz) Females: 260g (9oz)
Ringed Teal (Callonetta leucophrys)		In captivity in England, nests from spring through to autumn Little studied in the field Males: 190-360g (7-13oz) Females: 197-310g (7-11oz)
Carolina or North American Wood Duck (Aix sponsa)		Starts laying in March in Florida (later in the northern parts) and always ceases before mid-summer Nests in tree-holes or boxes Clutch size: 9-14 eggs, usually 12 Males: 539-879g (av. 680g) (1lb 8oz) Females: 482-879g (av. 539) (1lb 3oz)

COMMON NAME (Scientific)	HABITAT	BREEDING & WEIGHT
Mandarin Duck (A. galericulata)		In China, nesting occurs between late April — July Nests in tree-holes or boxes Clutch size: 9-10 eggs Both sexes: 444-550g (1lb 3½oz)
Australian Wood Duck or Maned Goose (Chenonetta jubata)		Breeds from spring (September — November) through summer and into autumn Clutch size: 9-11 eggs Males: 700-953g (av. 815g) (1lb 13oz) Females: 662-984g (av. 800g) (1lb 12oz)
Brazilian Teal (Amazonetta brasiliensis)		Breeding season extends beyond summer solstice Clutch size: 6-8 eggs Males: 340-480g (13½oz—1lb 1oz) Females: 350-90g (12—14oz)
Blue or Mountain Duck (Hymenolaimus malacorhynchos)		Begins nesting in October and November, but can last from August — January Clutch size: 4-9 eggs, usually 5 A long fledgling period Males: 753-1077g (av. 887g) (1lb 15oz) Females: 680-850g (av. 750g) (1lb 10½oz)
Torrent Duck (Merganetta armata)		In Andes, lays during August In Chile and Argentina, in wet period Clutch size: 3-4 eggs Males: 440g (about 15½oz) Females: 315-400g (11-12oz)
Salvadori's Duck (Salvadorini [Anas] waigiuensis)		Nests in May — October Clutch size: 3 eggs Males: 400-525g (av. 462g) (1lb) Females: 490-500g (av. 469g) (1lb ½oz)

COMMON NAME (Scientific)	HABITAT	BREEDING & WEIGHT	COMMON NAME (Scientific)	HABITAT	BREEDING & WEIGHT
DABBLING DUCKS (Tribe Anatini)			Baikal Teal (A. formosa)		Starts laying in June in captivity in UK; lasts from May — July in wild Clutch size: 6-9 eggs Males: 360-520g (av. 437g) (15½oz) Females: 402-505g (av. 431g) (15oz)
African Black (Anas sparsa)		Lays July — December in SW Cape Springtime (March — May) in UK in captivity Clutch size: 4-8 eggs Males: unreported Females: 952-1077g (2lb 1½oz — 2lb 6oz)	Northern Green-winged (including the European) Teal (A. crecca)		Pairing occurs mid-March, laying from mid-April Clutch size: 8-10 eggs Males: av. 360g (15oz) Females: av. 340g (12oz)
Chiloe Wigeon (A. sibilatrix)		Late March — late August (at Slimbridge, UK) In southern summer, they breed between August & January Clutch size: 5-8 eggs Males: av. 939g (2lb 1oz) Females: av. 828g (1lb 13oz)	Sharp-winged, Chilean and Speckled Teal (A. flavirostris)		Nesting occurs from late August — December depending on area Clutch size: 5-8 eggs Males: av. 429g (15oz) Females: av. 394g (14oz)
European or Common Wigeon (A. penelope)		Females nest at the end of their first year of life. Nests well hidden, laying mid-April & May Clutch size: 8-9 eggs Males: (in winter) 465-970g (av. 720g) (1lb9½oz) Females: 415-800g (av. 640g) (1lb 6½oz)	Cape Teal or Cape Wigeon (A. capensis)		Long season, nesting concentrated between August — November Clutch size: 5-11 eggs Males: 352-502g (av. 419g) (15oz) Females: 316-451g (av. 380g) (13½oz)
American Wigeon or Baldpate (A. americana)		Lays mid-May — early June Clutch size: 7-9 eggs Males: av. 770g (1lb 11oz) Females: av. 680g (1lb 8oz)	Grey Teal (including the Andaman Teal) (A. gibberifrons)		In Australia, nesting controlled by rains In NZ, lays from August — November Clutch size: 7-9 eggs Males: 395-670g (av. 507g) (1lb 2oz) Females: 350-602g (av. 474g) (1lb 1oz)
Falcated Duck (A. falcata)		Nests in USSR in May — June; in China, in May Clutch size: 6-9 eggs Males: 590-770g (av. 713g) (1lb 9oz) Females: 422-700g (av. 585g) (1lb 4½oz)	Bernier's or Madagascan Teal (A. bernieri)		As yet undescribed No records
Gadwall (A. strepera)		Nests from early May — mid-June Clutch size: 10 eggs Males: av. 990g (2lb 3oz) Females: av. 850g (1lb 14oz)			

COMMON NAME (Scientific)	HABITAT	BREEDING & WEIGHT
Chestnut-breasted or Chestnut Teal (*A. castanea*)		In Victoria, breeding occurs from June — December with a concentrated period during October Clutch size: 7-10 eggs Males: 340-708g (av. 595g) (1lb 5oz) Females: 368-737g (av. 539g) (1lb 3oz)
Brown Teal (including Auckland Islands and Campbell Island) (*A. aucklandica*)		Lays between July — December in New Zealand Clutch size: 5-7 eggs Female Auckland Islands Teal: around 450g (about 1lb) Female Brown Teal: 600g (1lb 5oz)
Mallard (including Greenland, Hawaiian, Mexican, Mottled and Florida ducks) (*A. platyrhynchos*)		Begins display in mid-October; laying occurs from March in UK Mallard Clutch size: 9-10 eggs Males: av. 1200g (2lb 10oz) Females: av. 1084g (2lb 3oz)
Laysan Teal (*A. laysanensis*)		Probably lays year round Nests hidden under bushes or in grass lumps near lagoon Clutch size: 5 eggs Males: av. 445g (1lb) Females: av. 450g (1lb)
American Black Duck (*A. rubripes*)		All first-year females attempt to nest but less than 10% breed successfully Lays mid-April — early June Clutch size: 9-10 eggs Males: av. 1330g (2lb 14½oz) Females: av. 1160g (2lb 8½oz)
Meller's Duck (*A. melleri*)		Breeding occurs from July — September Clutch size: av. 8 (5-13) in captivity Males: av. 940g (2lb 1oz) Females: av. 925g (2lb)

COMMON NAME (Scientific)	HABITAT	BREEDING & WEIGHT
Yellow-billed Duck (*A. undulata*)		In Southern regions, June — September; otherwise during wet season Clutch size: 4-10 eggs, usually 8 Males: 678-1208g (av. 954g) (2lb 2oz) Females: 630-1114g (av. 817g) (1lb 13oz)
Spot-billed Duck (*A. poecilorhyncha*)		China, Japan, USSR April — June Clutch size: 7-9 eggs (India) Males: 1230-1500g (2lb 11oz-3lb 5oz) Females: 790-1360g (1lb 12oz-3lb)
Grey or Pacific Black Duck (*A. superciliosa*)		July — October in southern Australia; March — May in north, and in NZ from September — January Clutch size: av. 9 eggs (Australia, NZ) Males: 765-1275g (1lb 11oz — 2lb 13oz) Females: 623-1275g (1lb 6oz — 2lb 13oz)
Philippine Duck (*A. luzonica*)		No nests studied in the wild, but springtime layer in captivity in UK Males: 803-977g (av. 906g) (2lb) Females: 725-818g (av. 779g) (1lb 11oz)
Bronze-winged or Spectacled Duck (*A. specularis*)		Long season. September—January in wild. Eggs laid between February and September in UK where three clutches a year of 4-6 eggs Females: av. 960g (2lb 2oz)
Crested Duck (*A. specularioides*)		Extended season, September — February Clutch size: 5-8 eggs Males: 1070-1180g (2lb 5½oz-2lb 9½oz) Females: av. 900g (2lb)

COMMON NAME (Scientific)	HABITAT	BREEDING & WEIGHT
Pintail (A. acuta)		Starts courting in December Lays from mid-April—June Clutch size: 8 or 9 eggs Males: 710-1250g (av. 850g) (1lb 14oz) Females: 585-935g (1lb 5oz—2lb 7oz)
Yellow-billed, Brown or Chilean Pintail (A. georgica)		Time of nesting varies depending on location, between October and December Clutch size: 4-10 eggs Males: 610-60g (1lb 5½oz—1lb 7oz) Females: 460-510g (1lb—1lb5½oz)
Bahama, Galapagos or White-cheeked Pintail (A. bahamensis)		Lays year-round Clutch size: 6-10 eggs Males: 474-533g (1lb1oz—1lb 3oz) Females: 505-633g (1lb 2oz—1lb 6oz)
Red-billed Pintail or Red-billed Teal (A. erythrorhyncha)		In Zimbabwe lays February — April In captivity in England, April — July Clutch size: 5-12 eggs Males: 503-755g (av. 617g) (1lb 6oz) Females: 434-786g (av. 566g) (1lb 4oz)
Silver or Versicolor (including Puna) Teal (A. versicolor)		Long season. Nesting between September — January Clutch size: 7-10 eggs Males: av. 442g (1lb) Females: av. 373g (13oz) Puna male: av. 546-600g (11lb 3½oz)
Hottentot Teal (A. hottentota)		December through April in Zambia & South Africa; May — June in Rhodesia; May — August from Kenya to Malaysia Clutch size: 6-8 eggs Both sexes: 224-53g (8-9oz)
Garganey (A. querquedula)		Migrates to Britain in spring to breed in early May Clutch size: 8-9 eggs Males: 240-542g (8½oz—1lb 3oz) Females: 220-445g (8oz—1lb)
Blue-winged Teal (A. discors)		Starts laying in late March — late April Clutch size: 10-11 eggs Males: 273-410g (av. 360g) (13oz) Females: 266-375g (av. 332g) (12oz)
Cinnamon Teal (A. cyanoptera)		Late arrivers at breeding grounds Lays in May Clutch size: 9-10 eggs Males: av. 408g (14½oz) Females: av. 362g (13oz)
Argentine Red Shoveler (A. platalea)		Lays from September — November Clutch size: 5-8 eggs Males: av. 608g (1lb 5½oz) Females: av. 523g (1lb 2½oz)
Cape Shoveler (A. smithii)		Nests at anytime of the year Clutch size: 5-12 eggs Males: 550-830g (av. 688g) (1lb 8oz) Females: 480-690g (av. 597g) (1lb 5oz)
Australian and New Zealand Shovelers (A. rhynchotis)		In NZ, breeds October — January; in Australia, August — December Clutch size: 9-10 eggs Males: 570-852g (av. 667g) (1lb 7½oz) Females: 545-745g (av. 665g) (1lb 7½oz)

COMMON NAME (Scientific)	HABITAT	BREEDING & WEIGHT
Northern or Common Shoveler (*A. clypeata*)		Late arriver at breeding grounds laying from mid-May Clutch size: 9 or 10 eggs Males: 410-1100g (14½oz-2lb6½oz) Female: 420-768g (15oz-1lb11oz)
Pink-eared Duck (*Malacorhynchus membranaceus*)		Anytime of the year depending on water levels Clutch size: 6-8 eggs Incubation takes 26 days Males: 290-480g (av. 404g) (14½oz) Females: 272-423g (344g) (12oz)
Marbled Teal (*Marmaronetta angustirostris*)		Starts breeding as late as May until early July Clutch size: 7-14 eggs Males: 240-600g (8½oz-1lb 5oz) Females: 250-550g (9oz-1lb 3½oz)

DIVING DUCKS
(*Tribe Aythyini*)

COMMON NAME (Scientific)	HABITAT	BREEDING & WEIGHT
Pink-headed Duck (*Rhodonessa caryophyllacea*)		Now extinct Males: 793-990g (av. 935g) (2lb) Females: 840-1360g (1lb 14oz-3lb)
Red-crested Pochard (*Netta rufina*)		Lays mid-April — mid-June Clutch size: 8-10 eggs Males: about 1190g (about 2lb 6½oz) Females: about 1100g (about 2lb 6½oz)
Southern Pochard (*N. erythrophthalma*)		Nests in rainy season In captivity in England they lay about a week before vernal equinox; long breeding season Clutch size: 6-15 eggs Males: 600-977g (1lb 5oz—2lb 2½oz) Females: 533-1000g (1lb 3oz—2lb 3oz)

COMMON NAME (Scientific)	HABITAT	BREEDING & WEIGHT
Rosy-bill (*N. peposaca*)		In captivity in UK short, late spring season, hatching May — late July Clutch size: 10 eggs Males: av. 1181g (2lb 9½oz) Females: av. 1004g (2lb 3oz)
Canvasback (*Aythya valisineria*)		Lays mid-May — mid-June Clutch size: 9-10 eggs Males: 950-1600g (av. 1250g) (2lb 12oz) Females: 900-1530 (av. 1154g) (2lb 8½oz)
European or Common Pochard (*A. ferina*)		Lays early May — early July Clutch size: 6-9 eggs Males: 930-1100g (av. 998g) (2lb 3oz) Females: 900-995g (av. 947g) (2lb 1½oz)
Redhead (*A. americana*)		Low success rate in breeding and hatching Lays from May — late June Clutch size: 7-8 eggs Males: av. 1080g (2lb 6oz) Females: av. 1030g (2lb 4oz)
Ring-necked Duck (*A. collaris*)		Breeds between May & end of June in north western North America Clutch size: 8-9 eggs Males: av. 790g (1lb 12oz) Females: av. 690g (1lb 9oz)
Australian White-eye or Hardhead (*A. australis*)		Nests between October & November Clutch size: 9-12 eggs Males: 525-1100g (av. 902g) (2lb) Females: 530-1060g (av. 838g) (1lb 14oz)

COMMON NAME (Scientific)	HABITAT	BREEDING & WEIGHT
Baer's Pochard or Siberian White-eye (A. baeri)		Little studied Males: about 880g (1lb 15oz) Females: about 680g (1lb 8oz)
Common or Ferruginous White-eye (A. nyroca)		Nests very close to water Lays in May & June Clutch size: 8-10 eggs Males: 500-650g (av. 583g) (1lb 5oz) Females: 410-600g (av. 520g) (1lb 2½oz)
Madagascan White-eye (A. innotata)		Recently disappeared No record
New Zealand Scaup or Black Teal (A. novae-seelandiae)		Laying occurs between October and February Average clutch size: 5 eggs Males: 630-760g (av. 695g) (1lb 8½oz) Females: 545-900g (av. 610g) (1lb 5½oz)
Tufted Duck (A. fuligula)		Females breed at end of first year of life Lays from mid-May — June Clutch size: 8-11 eggs Males: 1000-1400g (av. 1116g) (2lb 7oz) Females: 1000-1150g (av. 1050g) (2lb 5oz)
Greater Scaup (A. marila)		Starts laying in late May Clutch size: 8-10 eggs Males: av. 1000g (2lb 3oz) Females: av. 900-1200g (2lb-2lb10oz)

COMMON NAME (Scientific)	HABITAT	BREEDING & WEIGHT
Lesser Scaup (A. affinis)		Lays late May — July Clutch size: 10 eggs Males: av. 850g ((1lb 14oz) Females: av. 800g (1lb 12oz)

EIDERS
(Tribe Somateriini)
Eiders lay at two years old

COMMON NAME (Scientific)	HABITAT	BREEDING & WEIGHT
Common or Northern Eider (Somaterina mollissima)		Nesting starts in Iceland in second half of May Clutch size: 4-6 eggs Pacific race: av. 2600g (5lb 12oz) European race: Males: av. 2220g (4lb 14oz) Females: av. 1915g (4lb 4oz)
King Eider (S. spectabilis)		Begins laying mid-June Clutch size: 4-5 eggs Males: 1530-2010g (3lb 6oz—4lb 6oz) Females: 1500-1870g (3lb 6oz—4lb 1oz)
Spectacled or Fischer's Eider (S. fischeri)		Lays in late spring, after 1 June Clutch size: 4-6 eggs Both sexes: av. 1630g (3lb 11oz)
Steller's Eider (S. [Polysticta] stelleri)		Nesting late, starts in June Clutch size: 6-8 eggs Both sexes: about 860g av. (1lb 14½oz)
Labrador Duck (Camptorhynchus labradorius)		Now extinct Males: 864g (1lb 14½oz) Females: 482g (1lb 1oz)

COMMON NAME (Scientific)	HABITAT	BREEDING & WEIGHT
SEADUCKS (Tribe Mergini) All Mergini sexually mature at two years old		
Harlequin (Histrionicus histrionicus)		Begins laying in late May Clutch size: usually 6 eggs Males: av. 680g (1lb 8oz) Females: av. 540g (1lb 3oz)
Long-tailed Duck or Old Squaw (Clangula hyemalis)		Lays late May Clutch size: 6-9 eggs Males: av. 800g (1lb 12½oz) Females: av. 650g (1lb 7oz)
Common or Black Scoter (Melanitta nigra)		Lays from late May onwards Clutch size: 6-8 eggs Males: av. 1100g (2lb 6½oz) Females: av. 950g (2lb 1½oz)
Surf Scoter (M. perspicillata)		Lays end of May into June Nests concealed under bushes Clutch size: 5-7 eggs Males: av. 1000g (2lb 3oz) Females: av. 900g (2lb)
White-winged or Velvet Scoter (M. fusca)		Begins laying in mid-June Clutch size: 8 or 9 eggs Males: 1500-1700g (3lb 4½oz — 3lb 12oz) Females: 1200-1600g (2lb 10oz — 3lb 8oz)
Bufflehead (Bucephala albeola)		Lays April onwards in tree-holes by pools, lakes and slow rivers Clutch size: 8-9 eggs Males: av. 450g (1lb 1oz) Females: av. 330g (11½oz)

COMMON NAME (Scientific)	HABITAT	BREEDING & WEIGHT
Barrow's Goldeneye (B. islandica)		Breeds from mid-May onwards in tree holes or, in Iceland, in ground cavities Clutch size: 8-11 eggs Males: 1190-1305g (2lb 10oz—2lb 14oz) Females: 735-905g (1lb 10oz—2lb)
Common Goldeneye (B. clangula)		Nests from mid-April onwards in tree holes Clutch size: 10 eggs (8-11) Males: av. 1000g (2lb 3oz) Females: av. 800g (1lb 12½oz)
Hooded Merganser (Mergus cucullatus)		Nests in tree holes in April & May Clutch size: 10 eggs Males: av. 680g (1lb 8oz) Females: av. 540g (1lb 3oz)
Smew (M. albellus)		Nests in tree holes from late April — early June Clutch size: 7-9 eggs Males: 540-935g (1lb 3oz— 2lb 1oz) Females: 515-650g (1lb 2oz— 1lb 7oz)
Brazilian Merganser (M. octosetaceus)		June — July nesting season No record of clutch size
Red-breasted Merganser (M. serrator)		Begins laying end of April in southern part of range, later in northern. Nests on ground Clutch size: 9-10 eggs Males: av. 1200g (2lb 10oz) Females: av. 925g (2lb 1oz)

COMMON NAME (Scientific)	HABITAT	BREEDING & WEIGHT
Scaly-sided or Chinese Merganser (M. squamatus)		Little studied in the wild
Goosander or Common Merganser (M. merganser)		Nests in early spring (end of March on) in cavities Clutch size: 9-10 eggs Males: av. 1600g (3lb 8oz) Females: av. 1200g (2lb 10oz)
Auckland Islands Merganser (M. australis)		Now extinct No record
STIFFTAILS (Tribe Oxyurini)		
Black-headed Duck (Heteronetta atricapilla)		Parasitic nester, laying between September — December Males: 434-680g (av. 515g) (1lb 2oz) Females: 470-720g (av. 565g) (1lb 4oz)
Masked Duck (Oxyura dominica)		Year-round depending on location; in Cuba, May — July; in Santa Lucia, up to October; southern Martinique and Paraguay, season extends into December Clutch size: 4-6 eggs Males: 369-449g (av. 406g) (14oz) Females: 298-393g (av. 339g) (12oz)

COMMON NAME (Scientific)	HABITAT	BREEDING & WEIGHT
Ruddy Duck (including the Columbian and Peruvian Ruddy) (O. jamaicensis)		Northern Ruddy is able to lay for an extended period from May beyond mid-summer Clutch size: 8 eggs Males: av. 550g (1lb 3½oz) Females: av. 500g (1lb 1½oz)
White-headed Duck (O. leucocephala)		Lays May — July Clutch size: 7 eggs Males: 553-865g (av. 737g) (1lb 13oz) Females: 539-631g (av. 593g) (1lb 5oz)
Maccoa (O. maccoa)		Laying season prolonged in South Africa June — April, with a peak between September — December Clutch size: 4-8 eggs Both sexes: 450g-700g (1lb — 1lb 9oz)
Argentine Ruddy, Blue-bill or Lake Duck (O. vittata)		Season lasts from mid-October to early January in eastern Argentina Clutch size: 3-5 eggs Both sexes: 550-675g (1lb 3½oz— 1lb 8oz)
Blue-billed Duck (O. australis)		In northern Victoria, October — March; in WA, September — November Clutch size: 5-6 eggs Males: 610-965g (av. 812g) (1lb 12½oz) Females: 476-1300g (av. 852g) (1lb 14oz)
Musk Duck (Biziura lobata)		Australian resident which breeds in Victoria, September — November; in WA August — November Clutch size: 1-3 eggs Males: av. 2398g (5lb 5oz) Females: av. 1551g (3lb 6½oz)

INTERNATIONALLY RENOWNED ORNITHOLOGIST, Professor Janet Kear, has spent most of her adult life among ducks, geese, and swans and as a result, she has become familiar with their every habit.

Professor Kear received a doctorate from Cambridge University in 1959 and joined the Wildfowl and Wetlands Trust as a research scientist, becoming the curator of Martin Mere in 1977, and Director of Centres in 1991. Her home is at Martin Mere in Lancashire, along with thousands of migrant wild ducks, geese and swans who also live at the internationally famous wetland.

During her fascinating career, Janet Kear has been editor of the British Ornithologists' Union journal *Ibis*, and has published many articles and books, including *The Hawaiian Goose, Man and Wildfowl,* and *Swans*. Professor Kear has been a member of several conservation and wildlife societies and is a member of the Nature Conservancy Council for England.

In 1991, Janet Kear became the first woman to be appointed President of the British Ornithologists' Union.

Opposite page: Chiloe Wigeon.

INDEX

Above: Pintail snoozing. Opposite: Female Grey Duck with ducklings.

Tim Fitzharris

Geoff Moon

Australian Wood Ducks in the woods.

Geoff Longford

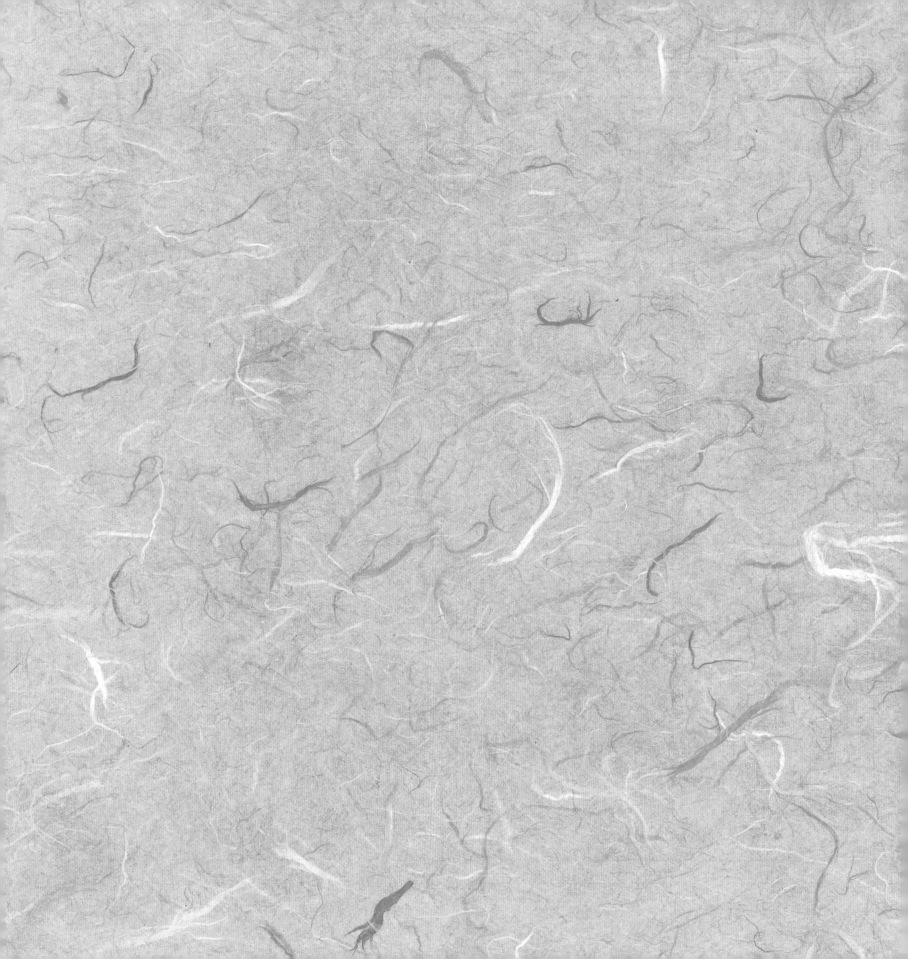